# Backroad Blessings

By Cassie Winner

Backroad Blessings

Copyright © 2023

Paperback ISBN: 978-1-63337-785-1
E-book ISBN: 978-1-63337-786-8

Cover and Internal Page layout by Melody Rittberger.

Printed in the United States of America.

# Backroad Blessings

By Cassie Winner

# Contents

# Contents Continued

# Prologue

ome on guys, I know you're tired but you have to keep going. You can't quit now, you're almost there. I know you're struggling, but it's the struggle that makes you stronger! As I yell these words, they grit their teeth, sweat is dripping down their faces. The slamming of the chains, the flipping of the tires, push up after push up, box jump after box jump, 3, 2, 1 stop, breathe and get a drink guys.

This is me, Cassie Winner. This is my life and this is what I do. I'm the proud mother of 2 wonderful boys, Mcgwire and Larkin and I'm married to my best friend, Patrick. I'm a Fitness Instructor and Personal Trainer and I'm loving every minute of it. I wouldn't have it any other way. This is just an example of one of my workout classes. As my class ends and I give each person a high five as they leave, I feel the presence of God all around me. I give my all to each workout I instruct because I know God placed me here and this is for His glory. Even though I write these workouts they are not fully from me but from God, who uses me and works through me.

At some point each person debated about walking into my class not knowing what to expect or if they could even do it, but here they are giving it all they've got and not giving up. I always tell them walking through the door is the first and hardest step. I know getting up and moving forward into something that is unfamiliar and new is scary but once they get here they have overcome the worst part. That's what this story is about, stepping into something new. When I started on this path I was led here by God.

The story I'm about to tell you is about walking down a path but suddenly being redirected a different way. It's about the love of a mother fighting for her sick child and how a family breaks apart but gets molded back together. It's about losing control of the situation and having nothing left, being at the bottom of yourself and knowing you can't do it on your own. It's about finding a safe place to go and finding the weapons to fight back. It's about finally dropping to your knees and handing everything over to God. It's how a family finds the goodness of God and keeps going. It's about never letting go of God's hand as He guides you through the rough waters and keeping your eyes on Jesus.

I yell these words in my class because I once lived them. I use the scars from my battle to encourage others to keep going and to not give up. I want to encourage you to keep moving forward and not look back. If you're reading this book today and you're struggling right now, it's ok. There's hope and believe me, you will make it. My goal through this book is to help guide you down a new path you are heading towards.

God allowed a storm in your life to prepare you for something bigger and better. You may be struggling right now but you are training for something that's going to make you stronger. Get ready because I see great things in your future. You might not see what I see because you're probably navigating through the dark, but grab a flashlight and let's explore down this old backroad. I want to help you find your path so you too can find your backroad blessing.

# CHAPTER 1

# The Backroad

It was a cold winter day as I looked out the window, snow was lightly falling and any other day the snow would look beautiful to me, but not that day. I couldn't see past the fog of the storm I was up against. I couldn't see the beauty in anything. It was a hard day for me, I felt empty, lost and alone. I was in a trance the whole morning, just staring off into space. I was there, but at the same time I wasn't there. I needed to run.

Running helps clear my mind and escape from all the chaos. I wasn't trying to run from my problems, I just needed an outlet. I couldn't just stay in the house. I hate to say it, but the house had too many reminders of the storm we were up against. I decided I had to get out for a little bit. I would be back, and I would be brave and face the storm again but I needed to reset myself. I got dressed, grabbed my shoes, my phone and put on my earbuds. I stepped outside and it was so cold, but I didn't care. I took in a deep breath of the cold crisp air, it hurt when I inhaled it and I could see my breath as I exhaled.

I looked around at my property and glanced at my children's pirate ship treehouse and remembered the days we played like we were pirates on it and pretended to fish off the side of it. I remembered when I used to push my oldest son McGwire on the rope swing. His sparkling blue eyes would light up and he would yell higher, mommy, higher. My eyes began to tear up, but I quickly wiped them away. I didn't want to cry, I've done enough of that. I started walking down the driveway and glanced at our family tree where we spray painted our initials, PW+CW+MW+LW. My heart sank. That was the only surviving tree when we cleared the property to build our house. We decided to keep it and it grew with us. Everything I looked at was wrapped with surrounding memories which was the reason why I needed to get out of the house.

I started running down the driveway to clear my head. My legs felt so heavy as if I was running through mud, but nothing compared to how heavy my chest felt. I had so much weighing on me. My family had so much going on at that moment. I already felt tired even though I had just started, but I was tired before I began. I didn't have much energy with everything I had going on but I wasn't going to quit. As I ran, I looked up at the sky and it gave me a sense of peace and clarity. There's something special about the sky and such a mystery behind the clouds. If only I could look deeper into the clouds, what would I see?

As I continued to run, it was a struggle to put one foot in front of the other. I was exhausted and felt numb but it wasn't from the cold. I was numb because of the pain deep inside of me. The snow was coming down harder as I ran. I may have been running through a snowstorm but it didn't compare to the storm I was up against at home. My oldest son McGwire was sick and there wasn't anything I could do about it. I tried everything imaginable, but nothing worked. I was angry, deeply angry at myself for not being able to stop his suffering, but I was also angry at God for allowing this to happen and for not healing him.

I found myself not wanting to run anymore as my feelings overwhelmed me. I wanted to turn around and go back, but I had to keep moving forward even though it hurt. I couldn't quit, not now. I was getting closer to where I was headed. My mind just wouldn't shut down, my thoughts were getting the best of me, my struggles were consuming me.

I hit that old gravel road, hitting those sharp jagged rocks was a checkpoint for me. Turning onto this backroad gave me clarity and it kept me moving forward. There was a huge hill I had to run down so I just let my legs loose, opened up my arms like a bird feeling the cold air hit my fingertips as I soared down the hill. I let the hill take me and I used the momentum to coast up the next hill. Then I reached the big hill that felt more like a mountain. I didn't feel strong enough to make the climb, but I knew what awaited me at the top. I gritted my teeth and drove my knees up and pushed as hard as I could. I wasn't stopping now.

As I reached the top of the hill I knew I was finally there. My legs were so weak. I stopped suddenly in my snow covered footprints and I fell to my knees while breathing rapidly. My heart was pounding out of my chest as I whispered under my breath, "I'm here, I made it." A tear formed in the corner of my eye and I wiped it away and said it louder, "I'm here God, I made it!" I couldn't hold back my emotions any longer and completely fell apart and cried until I couldn't cry anymore. I was depleted and God knew it, but he brought me here for a reason. That backroad was my outlet. You could call it my safe place, because it's where I found God. I could feel His presence. This place to me is "Paradise" and that's what I named it.

You may ask why I'm telling you this. The answer to your question is, you need this illustration to know where my journey began. This is the road that led me to God. I've known who God is my entire life. I was raised going to church every Sunday, but I didn't truly know Him until my son was sick. It may be an old dirt road to some, but to me it's more than that. This road represents so much more than cardio alone, it's my escape from those days when I'm not okay. I want you to know, it's okay not to be okay sometimes. You're going to have days that are too hard to handle on your own.

My advice to you is when you're having a bad day, take all your pain to God and He will give you His peace. Find a safe place you can escape to and use that time to talk to Him one on one. Sometimes we need to step out of the darkness of the world and find a little piece of heaven to step into.

That's what this story is about. It's about that long winding road that you can't get to the end of. Or it's that door that you reach for but you can't quite open. It's about a random back road with lots of twists and turns that end up going nowhere. I don't know your story but I do know maybe that you're lost like I was, maybe you're hurting and you're scared, I understand, I get it, I was too. Like I said, my oldest son was so sick, he was tired and so was I.

My family was emotionally drained. I didn't want to see him like this anymore, I wanted him to be better, I wanted it all to be over but it was far from it. I was supposed to be the mother that could fix everything, but I couldn't fix this, it was too big for me. I wanted it to be me that was sick and not him, I wanted to take it from him so he didn't have to suffer anymore, so I ran that day. I ran to my Heavenly Father. I didn't run to that backroad to run away from my problems, I ran there to the One who was bigger than my problems. I had to hand my child over to God, which is so hard to do, but I had to let go and let God take over. When your child is sick, it's an emotional navigating challenge, one that I wasn't ready for, but we never are. I was so weak and vulnerable.

At one point while writing this story, I hesitated about sharing this moment because anyone who knows me knows that I don't like to show my weakness, but why? Why don't we want to reveal our weaknesses? I ask myself these questions now because today I know my weakness could be someone else's strength and I want to help give you strength to get back up. Maybe you're vulnerable and in a dark place like I was. Is this you? If so, I want to help shine some light on you and tell you it's going to be okay. There will be light around the corner, but sometimes you have to navigate through the dark to be able to find it. That light is God, He is your path and He wants to show you the way. Jesus is the way, so follow Him. It might be a bumpy road but you will get there to finally see what He has been trying to show you.

I tell you this because I was in the dark and found the light and I'm a changed person because of it. When you're struggling, how do you rise up from something that feels like it has already defeated you? How do you endure something that feels like it's never ending? How do you wake up knowing you have to walk another day with heavy legs? How do you face another day that is harder than yesterday?

My answer to these questions is Jesus. You can and will overcome this with Jesus guiding you. You can still walk even if you have a little limp. You can still talk even if you have a little stutter. You can still work even if you have a little shake to your hands. You have to stop focusing on what's wrong and look at what's right. You have to look at things a little differently, in a different perspective. Maybe you have to squint a little harder, and if you look at it just right, you might see the blessing behind the storm. Being lost is my story, the backroad is my testimony, the run was my healing. I may have been lost on an old gravel road but that road was my journey of how I was found. That may not make sense right now but stick with me and you'll see, because seeing isn't believing, but believing is seeing. I never understood that expression until I was put in a situation that I couldn't dig my way out of. I was stuck in "the Pit" but "the Pit" is what opened my eyes.

# CHAPTER 2

# The Pit

What is "The Pit"? It's those moments in your life when you're having a hard time, you feel stuck, you feel hopeless and don't believe in yourself anymore. Some people fall into "The Pit" and never get back out, they just sink further down. It might feel like you're stuck and there's no way out, but in reality there is a way. I was in " The Pit ", I was deep in it, but I found my way out. "The Pit" wasn't designed to get stuck in, it was designed to help you grow stronger. I believe I'm stronger today because of it. Getting out is where your journey begins. My advice to everyone is don't settle, don't give up, it's not over, it's only just begun. You may have found yourself in a difficult time of your life, whether it's family issues, insecurities, sickness, addictions, self doubt or finances, but don't let "The Pit" win. Don't let it consume you because you were made to win, VICTORY is yours.

The battles we go through don't last, they were placed on our path to build us up to be the people we were made to be. God may have allowed me to fall into "The Pit" to help me grow, but He pulled me out before it defeated me. The pit made me strong. God allows you to fall because He wants to use you, but first He needs to train you.

Our successes in life and our true purposes are disguised as a struggle but in reality our struggles are placed on us to prepare us for how God will use us. It doesn't matter why you're in the pit, what matters is you get out and God wants to help you. God helps all, heals all, and loves all. God's hand was there reaching to pull me out, the problem was I never reached back for it. I thought I could do it on my own. I didn't try, so instead I sank deeper. It wasn't until I opened my eyes to see God's hand and realized I couldn't do it on my own. I finally took His hand and fought back. Sometimes we have to go farther down into the pit before we realize we have help. God has been there with open arms, we can't forget about Him, he is Our Father, he breathed life into us, we have to have faith in him, he isn't going to forsake us. He loves us. I've had hard times, my life has been tested and turned upside down, but it's how you handle it that makes all the difference in the world.

God hit pause in my life. He slowed me down. I was scared, lost and not sure if I would find my way out but I did. Sometimes we need someone to hit pause in our lives because we become programmed and we act as if we are robots. We are functioning but no longer feeling. We become cold and we forget we are people with feelings of love and happiness, not bitterness. Don't take life for granted, live life to the fullest, but not to the point that you take your body and make it become a machine. Slow down and breathe before God has to do it for you. Overcome "The Pit" because we will all face it one way or another and this is how I began my journey of my backroad blessing. It was a long run but that run is how I became the true me that God created. Let me take you back a few years and show where God hit pause in my life, but first before we do that, let's explore where it all began down the old gravel road.

# CHAPTER 3

# Paradise

anger was my best friend, my pal, my first child. Well kind of my first child, he was our first dog. He was the best dog in the world. When my husband Patrick and I were looking for a dog and we saw Ranger, we knew he was the one we needed. He went everywhere with us and we did so much with him. The day we had to put him down, I was broken because my running journey began with him. I was not an avid runner but Ranger and I explored, we ran a little and we also went on long hikes through the woods. The woods we explored were so special but they were not the same without him. When he passed away it was hard to run in the woods again, I felt empty and Patrick knew the sadness it brought me.

Patrick decided to surprise me one day and took my family and I on a little drive in the side by side to show me a road he found for me to run on. To be honest, I didn't like that old gravel road at first. There was a gigantic hill to climb in the first couple minutes of running. I looked at him and said, " You gotta be kidding me. Do you see that monster hill I have to climb?" He smiled and said, "Yep!" I looked at it again and I wasn't feeling that hill, I didn"t like running up hills but I did it anyway just to pacify Patrick. When I got to the top, I was completely out of breath but when I came around the corner, there it was, Paradise. Patrick and our boys were on top waiting for me. Patrick knew I was mesmerized by this place. He said, " It was worth the climb wasn't it." I smiled and said, "Yes it was, it's so beautiful here, thank you!" Patrick said, "I knew you would like it." I gave him a big hug and kiss and said, "You know me so well."

I continued running on that road and the hills got a little easier each time. Little did I know that road was going to have a deeper meaning to it later on. The purpose of me telling you this is, it's important you know the background on that road for me and how it all started. It's my outlet that I run to on the hard days. It's my safe place that makes me happy. One thing to consider is that sometimes your safe place might not look as it seems. You may not like it at first. It might be hidden behind a hill that you don't want to climb, but just keep climbing because you will discover something special beyond those hills. To get up those hills though, you will need to have good endurance.

What is endurance? By definition, endurance is the power of enduring an unpleasant or difficult situation without giving up. I love running, Why do I love running? I mean really, running is hard, and it's not fun in a lot of people's opinions. People ask me all the time, why do you enjoy running? They can't understand or comprehend it. I used to hate running with a passion so I understand why they ask me these questions. Through the years as I explored running, it became a tool for me. Running is my weapon, it's my escape from the world. Running is mindless and that's what I love about it because my head is always thinking but this is my way to turn it off. My question to you is, what is your outlet? What do you love to do? What makes you happy? You have to find it. I know running is painful so how could I enjoy it?

You could say I adopted one painful thing for another. Why would I substitute one kind of pain for a different kind? I don't know why. I guess it's kind of like this, if your foot hurts, maybe if you pinch your arm it will distract you from your foot hurting. Crazy, right? Maybe, but I guess the pain of running blocks the pain I struggle with in life. One thing I do know is, when I was up against a storm in my life, my escape from that was putting on my shoes and going for a run. Life represents endurance just like running does. Sometimes when we are up against something hard in our lives, we have to learn how to endure it and walk through it one step at a time. Life is a roller-coaster with lots of ups and downs. Sometimes we face "I'm on top of the world moments" but other times we face a downhill challenge, as if the world is crashing down on us. Although it feels terrible to run up a hill, you gain something from it. Running uphill makes you feel strong when you reach the top. You gain confidence and the view on top says it all.

All the hard work pays off at the end. It's the same with life, we have to work for it. It takes one step at a time to get to the top and when you get there you experience the same "I'm on top of the world moment". When you're running down a hill, although it's easier, you won't gain much from it. Honestly running down a hill you are more likely to get injured, lose control and fall. As a runner, falling is a major setback. In life, it's the same way. When life is too easy we take the easy road and find ourselves getting too close to the edge and when we fall it's much harder to climb out of the pit we fell into. Why do I run? Because if I run I learn how to endure pain that life might throw at me and I know God can help me endure it.

What I am saying is we have to keep putting one foot in front of the other moving forward, because each step we take leads us to victory. I run so I can face the challenges in life and learn how to endure uncomfortable moments in life. I know what pain feels like and maybe you are in pain right now. I want you to know that there's hope, so don't give up. Find your outlet to help you endure life's dark moments so you too can experience the "I'm on top of the world moments!"

# CHAPTER 4

# Storms

I will be talking a lot about storms in this book. We all know what a storm looks like. A storm can suddenly come out of the blue. Dark clouds develop, the wind picks up, the temperature drops and rain, thunder and lightning sets in. The storms that I will be talking about in this book are just like that. It's those moments in your life where it feels dark and cold and the wind knocks you off your feet and it makes you take cover and hide.

Real actual storms can be scary but they don't compare to the storms of life. God is always working in our life and He's always around, taking care of you in the midst of the storm. A lot of things that happen in our lives feel like a storm, but if you think back to the storm in your life, doesn't it feel like the storms we faced are the biggest memories we hold closest to our hearts? Some of our biggest blessings in life can be disguised as storms and some of the biggest storms make for the best stories. One of my greatest memories revolves around an actual storm. It's about riding through a rainstorm and never looking back and this is how it all started.

One day my youngest son, Larkin, was riding his bike up and down the driveway as fast as he could. Then suddenly, one training wheel broke off his bike and the other was just hanging there but he kept going anyway. It didn't phase him. We all laughed and I looked at my husband and said, "I don't think he needs the training wheels anymore." A couple days later we decided to go on a family bike ride. Larkin was excited. He was finally free from the training wheels. It's funny thinking back on it, because those training wheels were something that he thought he needed but they were actually the things that were holding him back.

God will sometimes remove things from our lives that we feel we need but in reality, they're things that have been holding us back. When we first started our bike ride, it was beautiful outside. The sun was shining and there was a light breeze in the air. We were enjoying our time together as a family. We were laughing and talking until suddenly, the weather started to change. Halfway through our bike ride the wind picked up and a big rain cloud started to develop out of nowhere. I said to Patrick,"Do you think we should turn around and go back?" Patrick stopped and pulled his phone and looked at the radar and said, "It looks like it's going to rain a little but it's not going to last long. I think we'll be ok if we keep going. If it starts raining, there's a shelter coming up that we can stand under until it passes." As we worked towards the shelter, it started to sprinkle.

Then suddenly the rain picked up and started to come down harder. In an instant we were soaked but in the distance we could see the shelter. It was an old gas station. We quickly pedaled to it and made it safely under the shelter. Larkin said "Mommy your hair is wet." I was drenched and looked like I came straight out of the shower. Through that short amount of time waiting for the storm to pass, we talked, and laughed. Something we didn't always take the time to do because our lives were so busy.

God put our day on pause for a few minutes and we had to stop in the midst of the storm because it got too strong for us. God placed us under the shelter and gave us a moment together to talk and enjoy each other. God gave us a memory.

I don't remember all of our bike rides, but that storm has allowed me to remember this one. As the storm passed, McGwire and Larkin were ready to go again. It was still sprinkling a little but we took off on our bikes anyway. We could have ridden back to our truck and went home but our day wasn't over yet. My kids found some puddles and began to ride through them splashing each other as they rode as fast as they could through them. Some guy pulled over in his truck while he was eating his lunch and found us very entertaining. He was laughing as we raced by him.

Soon the sun peeked through the clouds and created a beautiful sky and the storm was over, but the memory was made. Don't miss your miracle by giving up in the middle of your storm. We could have stopped and gone back home but we rode through the storm. Sometimes it's the staying power we need to find the miracle hidden behind the storm. It's easy to get excited when you finally find that breakthrough or finally receive your healing. Just don't forget what it was like when you were getting the testimony that you are now giving.

I know you may be up against your storm right now and it's not that easy. I promise when you ride through the puddles, you might get wet, just remember the storm won't last, but you will. You'll walk out of your storm stronger and you will turn those dark clouds into rainbows.

# CHAPTER 5

# Larkin Winner

It's important you know who we are as a family, so I'm going to share a little background to help you fully understand our story and understand how God works through people. Sometimes He reveals our purpose in baby steps throughout our lives. I think it's important that you see how God used my family when we were up against the storm of our lives. God is going to use you too and your storm has purpose behind it, but you have to keep riding through it.

I'm going to start with my youngest son, Larkin Winner. You have to love Larkin. He is 6 years old and is currently in kindergarten. He's full of pure joy, adventure, spontaneity, into everything, and leaving evidence behind. He's the one you have to watch carefully. He's messy and destructive, but lots of fun. Full of personality and character, he's my ornery one. Aside from all of that, he's full of compassion. His heart is bigger than he can contain.

In preschool, I began to get messages about him not paying attention in class and not focusing. That didn't surprise me much, and I wasn't too concerned because I knew who my boy was. He's my curious one that is always paying attention to the things going around him rather than the things in front of him. One day Larkin was playing in the sandbox with a friend at school and they decided it would be a good idea to put sand in their pockets so they could bring some home to play with. That's my Larkin, but there's a different and deeper side to him that I believe God uses.

One day I was helping in his class for Valentine's Day and I noticed a boy drop all his art supplies on the floor. He dropped everything, pens, pencils, markers, books and all. They went crashing to the floor and Larkin was across the room from him and noticed what had happened. Without hesitation he came to the boy's rescue and picked everything up for him. That's my son. Yeah, he's my ornery one but at the end of the day, he will always come to your rescue.

On another occasion I received another message from Larkin's preschool teacher. I pulled it up to read and began thinking, oh no, what did he do today, but it was different this time. There was a new girl in his class and they were in line and Larkin was the caboose or the tail end of the line. His job was to make sure no one drifted away from the line. The new girl stopped as the line kept moving. Larkin noticed her drift away and he made the tough decision to leave the line to go after her. The teacher noticed both of them were missing. Panic set in with her. She began looking around and Larkin and the girl were nowhere to be seen. Suddenly she saw Larkin and the little girl coming around the corner. Larkin was holding her hand guiding her back safely to the line. He did his job and his teacher was so relieved. His teacher said she will never forget that moment.

Larkin has already had so much impact in people's lives and he is only 6 years old. When McGwire was so sick, and I was so consumed in taking care of him, I felt like I lacked taking care of Larkin the way I wanted to. God showed me that Larkin took the storm we were up against and rolled with it. He has known God his whole life, because when we finally found God in our storm, Larkin was 1 year old.

Now, another story that I am going to tell you about him carries a lot of significance to my point of how God uses people and I believe He chose to use Larkin a lot. Wednesdays were Mommy and Larkin days. He was off on Wednesday from preschool, so I cleared my schedule so we could have our special day together and I cherished those days. We always went on an adventure.

One Wednesday morning, it was a beautiful day so Larkin and I took off for the day. We were hiking and he came across some old broken pieces of 2x4 wood. He grabbed them and started putting them in a pile. I watched him and smiled and said, "What are you doing bud?" He looked at me with those chocolate brown eyes and said "I'm collecting wood Mommy". I said, "That's cool." "Do you need some help pal?" He said "Yes". " We need more wood like this," I said "Ok, what are we going to do with it?" "Are we going to build a house?"

He smiled and said, "No Mommy." "This wood is the only way to get to heaven." I looked at him and smirked, I said, "It is?" He smiled and said, "Yes." I bent down to his level and looked deep into his eyes and said, "Ok bud, then lets collect more wood." He said, "I need one more piece." I said, "Well, let's go find it."

We hiked around looking for one more piece and finally there it was. It was an identical piece of the same wood that he has been collecting. Larkin grabbed it and put it in his pile and said, "There, we're done." I said, "Ok great, we did it pal!" We gave each other a high five. I looked at our pile and said, "Now what?" "Should we build something with it?" He said, "Daddy can. Can we bring it home?" I said, "Let's ask daddy about it and maybe we can come back and get it later." He said, "Okay". I looked down at my watch and said, "Well, it's about time to go pick up bubby from school." Larkin was always excited when it was time to get McGwire from school, he missed his big brother.

The next day my husband and I decided to go for a walk. I told him about mine and Larkins adventure. We were close to the spot where Larkin and I gathered the wood and I said, "Do you want to see Larkins pile of wood?" Patrick smiled and said "Sure." We walked over to the spot where he put the wood pile and it was still there right where we left it. My husband asked, "What did he say this wood was for?" I said, "Larkin said the wood was the only way to get to heaven. Patrick smiled and said," I wonder why he said that." and I replied, "I don't know but I love how his little mind works."

My husband picked up the wood and saw all the holes in it. Then something hit me right then and there and it must have triggered something in my husband's mind too. We started putting the pieces of wood together. We rearranged the wood in different ways until it was just right. We placed it with one hole on the bottom, one hole on the right side and one hole on the left side. We made a cross out of the broken pieces of wood. The holes were located in the same spots where Jesus's hands and feet were nailed to the cross. The cross we made symbolized Jesus and He is the only way to heaven. I couldn't believe the impact this had on me.

This little boy was 5 years old, but he already knew Jesus. We took the pieces home and my husband pieced them together and formed a cross. He engraved CRZFT in it. That is the logo for my gym, Crazee Fitness. We hung the cross in my gym and when Larkin got home we showed him and he smiled and was happy we brought it home.

The cross has such a deep meaning to me because I suffered a lot through the time my son McGwire was sick worrying about Larkin. He was only one when McGwire got sick. A lot of my attention went to McGwire and I hated that I couldn't be the mom I wanted to be to Larkin. The guilt that I carry about this can really bring me down. The cross I have hanging in my gym has helped me heal. It shows me that Larkin was never alone, God held him when I couldn't and that comforted me so much. God was holding Larkin's hand through all the chaos.

I read the Bible to my boys every night before bed. Larkin loves to draw so we got him a sketch book for Christmas. One night while I was reading the Bible to them, Larkin drew three crosses in his sketchbook. When I finished reading our passage for the evening I said, "What did you draw pal?" He said, "I drew three crosses mommy, Do you like them?" I hugged him and said, "I love them pal, they look really awesome."

I started to notice a trend of him drawing three crosses every night as I read the bible. One night he showed me his sketchbook and it was full of these drawings. I never understood what these three crosses meant. I knew on the day Jesus was crucified, there were two thieves, one on each side of Jesus. Then it hit me one day. I knew this wasn't by any accident that he was drawing these three crosses. There was a deeper meaning behind it. I knew God was working through him trying to deliver us a message. I needed to break this down a little further. God was calling me to study this passage with the boys.

One night while reading the bible to them, I decided we were going to read the passage about Jesus and the two thieves. I pulled it up and I read it. This is what it said. One thief said, "Jesus, remember me when you come into your kingdom." Jesus answered him, "Truly I tell you, today you will be with Me in paradise." Luke 23:42-43 NIV. When I read this, I realized God was speaking to me so I could speak to you at the time I was writing this book.

I had already written this chapter and had to come back and add this. It's important you know that Paradise is a real place and it awaits you, too. What exactly is Paradise? Paradise is often described as a higher place, a better place, a place where you can find peace. A heavenly place, a place of rest. Paradise is your happy place. One day we will be in heaven and that will be paradise, but until then God is calling you to find your paradise of this world, find your outlet.

God loves when you are spending time doing something that you love and doing it while you spend time with Him. As you know, I named my backroad that I run on, Paradise. God is calling you to rise up from the storm that you are in and go find a safe place. Find a place that brings you happiness and spend some time there.

The crosses Larkin drew, represent life. There is life after death but you have to carry your cross through the struggles of life, even when you don't think you can anymore. Don't give up. Never stop running this crazy race called life, because you will find peace and you will find your paradise. Just keep walking with me down this backroad and we will find your breakthrough. My paradise is some old rugged backroad, what's yours?

# CHAPTER 6

# Patrick Winner

L et's move on to my husband Patrick Winner. There is so much to say about him. He means the world to me. We have been through a lot together. Patrick is very humble, honest, loving, and completely spontaneous. He is game for anything, I mean anything. He's content, he doesn't get too excited.

Patrick operates well in scary situations. Nothing really phases him, if it does he never shows it. What goes on inside his mind, I really don't know. He has always been a mystery to me in that way. I guess that's hard for me to understand because my mind runs so fast and I have to speak it.

Patrick is the calm in all my storms. Patrick and I are opposites and maybe that's why we complement each other so well. He has taught me to stay grounded and settle. Countless times he has stopped me in my tracks when he sees me spinning out of control. I keep him moving so he doesn't get lost in the fast pace of life. Patrick is so good for me in so many ways and I believe I'm good for him too.

Patricks's my rock, my soulmate, and the love of my life. He was placed on my path for a reason. If it wasn't for him, I wouldn't be doing what I'm doing today. My husband believes in me more than I do. He's so compassionate, loyal, and trustworthy. He would do anything to make his family happy.

Patrick is a builder by trade but also the builder of my dreams. When I come up with crazy things in my head that any other man would roll his eyes at, he brings them to life. He has brought my dreams to surface and he never once doubted me. We were made for each other.

Through this story you will see the sacrifices he makes for the love of his family. I struggled a lot when my oldest son was so sick but he endured what I couldn't. He was a shoulder for me to cry on. He held me together when I was falling apart. When I broke to pieces, he put me back together. He was my strength when I was weak. When I finally gave in and dropped to my knees and surrendered, he dropped with me. If not for him, I would have never been able to rise from all of this. If not for him, I wouldn't be the woman I am today. He believed in me when I didn't. He never let me quit even when I wanted to and believe me, I wanted to so many times. He always refocused me and encouraged me when I needed it the most.

My gym is called CRAZEE FITNESS. I know that's an unusual name but it got its name because that's how it began. It started with crazy dreams and making crazy decisions but that's how it happens. You have to take a leap of faith and my husband helped me do that.

The start of my love for exercise all began when I first met Patrick. I met him in the cereal aisle at Krogers as he was stocking shelves. As I was trying to select a cereal, I looked from the corner of my eye at this young blue eyed boy stocking the shelves. Our eyes locked for a moment and I quickly turned my head and refocused on the cereal again and I gave him a second look and that was where it all began. When our eyes locked, we knew we were meant to be.

We went on our first date on the day after Christmas and we have been inseparable since then. One month later he signed up to go to bootcamp. I didn't want him to go and didn't know what would happen with us, but God kept us together through writing each other letters. Our relationship grew deeper through the words of that powerful pen.

When Patrick came back, our bond was even stronger than before. We went to college together, we were at the beginning of a new chapter. In our down time between classes we would spend time together. As time went by and we grew closer, he got the call we didn't want. He was being deployed. My heart broke knowing once again we were going to be separated. Losing him again was even harder this time because we were so close and I feared the worst of what could happen to him.

I had to continue this chapter of my life without him. I needed to find something to fill in the gap of Patrick being gone. I came across the college's gym. The gym filled the void of the absence of Patrick. I didn't know what I was doing in that gym. I never really worked out much so I migrated to the treadmill. I walked and jogged a little and the treadmill became therapy for me. I missed Patrick but I felt happy everytime I hit the gym. I explored a little more each time and would watch other people use the other machines and then I would try them out.

It was a small gym but at the time that's what I needed. When my husband returned home, I was thrilled. We were in different chapters but we merged them together and our roots became stronger. I introduced my husband to my gym. I was so excited to show him what I learned and he was happy to be there with me. He wanted to grow and explore a bigger gym, it was time for us to expand. We decided to get memberships at a bigger gym and he taught me how to use all the machines and free weights and that's where my roots started, this is where my journey in fitness began.

# CHAPTER 7

# Cassie Winner

W ho am I and all the factors that built me to be me?

First of all I'm just a girl with big dreams in the small town of Malta, Ohio. I grew up in Malta and currently live next door to where I grew up. The road I use to ride my bike up and down is the same road I get to watch my kids grow up on too. The beauty of it is, my parents live next door, you can't get any better than that.

If you know me, you will know that I am a yes girl. Anything you ask I will try to make it happen, even if it runs me ragged. Yes, I'm a people pleaser, I always have been. Letting one person down can keep me awake at night. I'm a person that feels like there is always a way to make something work and I will find that way. I feel if I say no, I'm letting someone down and I can't live with that. I never want to let one person slip through the cracks because they matter to me. Once they become a part of my life, I feel the compassion to help them.

I'm a person that if I put my mind to it, I will do it. I can't give up because giving up shows weakness and I don't like revealing that side of myself. I'm an overthinker. I often try too hard and sometimes because of that I fall short and when I do, it scares me. I don't want to lose control of anything, I have to be in control, because if I'm not, who will be. These are in some ways good qualities in a person but they can tend to be real problems and you will see why throughout my story.

Letting go is a problem for me and in this story God taught me, it's okay to let go. God has it all under control and it took a long time for me to figure that out. I had to learn that it doesn't all have to fall on me. I can lean on God but I have to trust Him and have faith. Maybe you can relate to this, maybe this is you too. If so, it's ok. These are good qualities, but we need to learn how to use them as our strengths and lay them down when we need to.

I went to school to be a mammographer, and I worked in that field for 10 years. How I was placed in this position, I really don't know, it just sort of happened. It wasn't my original plan. Being a mammographer wasn't the dream, but I guess you could say I was placed there for a reason. I believe being a mammographer was the stepping stone to prepare me for the path I am currently on today. I'm a very compassionate person, I always have been. I believe my mom is the reason for that.

My whole life my Mom has shown me what it looks like to help people. My Mom's heart has always been in the right place. I constantly saw her reach out to someone who was struggling. I saw the impact she had on people and I knew I wanted to help people like she did. My Mom has always been so good at listening and pouring out advice a person needs. Just watching her as a child do this, I knew what it took to be a compassionate person. My Mom didn't have to tell me because she showed me. That's why it's so important to watch what you say or do in front of your kids because they will more than likely do it too. Kids are sponges and I was able to soak that up.

My Mom was a stay at home Mom. Growing up, she was always there for my brother and I. When we were upset, we knew we could run to her. Mom has always been my lifeline and still is. I can remember since I was a little girl, I wanted to help people. It all started in kindergarten. I was sitting at my desk and a little boy in my class caught my attention. Even me being as young as I was, I could tell by looking at the boy he didn't have much. He came to school dirty, his hair was always sticking up and his clothes were too small for him. I could tell he didn't have a good home life and my little mind couldn't wrap my head around that, because I did. That being said, those reasons didn't make me shy away from him. It's actually quite the opposite, those were the reasons that drew me closer to him.

He didn't have any friends and I felt bad for him. I knew I needed to step up and become his friend. I knew he didn't have much and I didn't have much to offer but what I did have to offer was a friendship.

When it was nap time, I stretched my mat out beside his and we laid there and that's when I noticed his shoes. As he laid there and drifted to sleep, I laid there staring at his shoes. They were so dirty with holes in them and I knew he needed a new pair. This bothered me all day. Throughout the rest of the day, I kept looking at his shoes. I noticed his big toe was popping out of his shoe. I looked at my shoes, then I looked at his and I thought, mine looked so nice compared to his. I thought, this isn't fair. I wanted better for him.

When I got home from school and played for a little bit, mom called my dad, brother and me down for supper. The dinner table is where my family talked. We had some of our best conservations there. Mom asked my Dad how work went. Then she moved on to my brother talking about school and then finally it was my turn. She asked me how my day went. I told her about my day and then I asked if we could buy some new shoes for a boy in my class because he had holes in them. Mom and Dad said," We can't just buy him new shoes without asking his family first." I was disappointed because I wanted this for him.

My point to this story is, since I was little I had this unbearable feeling of the need to help others. It has been embedded into me my whole life. Maybe it was in the way I was raised or maybe God birthed this in me as a little girl. As I grew older and graduated highschool I had to make a decision about my future plans. My inspiration for that decision came from my cousin Carrie Weiner.

My cousin Carrie fought most of her life with the diagnosis of a brain tumor. She spent most of her time having surgeries and doing chemo and radiation. She sadly lost that battle when she was at the young age of 19. Losing her was hard on me, because I saw her on the holidays fighting these battles and not giving up and I wanted her to win the fight. She needed the win and she needed the victory. Carrie was a true fighter, she taught me what it took to fight. When we got the call she was going to pass, my heart sank. The reality of it hurt so bad.

When we went to see her one last time, the ride to her house was long and so hard for me. I remember staring out the car window just looking at the stars thinking, she will be up there soon. She will be in heaven, but I didn't want it to end like this. As we walked into her house, there were people everywhere. People I knew and people I didn't know.

My cousin was back in a bedroom and my family and I started to walk towards the room to go see her, but something suddenly stopped me from going. I couldn't do it. I didn't want to remember her like that. I wanted to remember her the way she was at my Grandma's house for all the holidays. I needed to remember all the good memories, not this. I was young and naive and I wasn't ready for death because I never really experienced seeing it yet. Especially with her being such a young woman. I chose not to go, so instead I ran outside to secretly cry. My aunt saw me run out the door and found me and hugged me. She said,'" You don't have to go see her, she knows you love her and she understands."

Later that evening my brother and I went home to stay at my cousin's house while Mom and Dad stayed with Carrie and her family that night. My brother, my cousin and I camped out on the living room floor. As I drifted off to sleep that night I had a dream. I was in my house sitting on the couch with my brother and cousin. In one of our chairs, I saw someone sitting there. I remember trying to figure out who it was. We were watching one of my favorite movies, Con Air.

I remember my eyes were locked on that person in the chair. I felt like I knew her but I couldn't figure out who she was. She had a sparkling green prom dress on with beautiful blonde hair. I remember her turning her head to look back at me and she smiled a big beautiful smile. That's when I realized the person in that chair was my cousin Carrie. As long as I can remember my cousin had a crooked smile due to the brain tumor and all of the surgeries she had. That night, in that dream, her smile wasn't crooked anymore. She had a big beautiful smile.

Suddenly I was awakened by my aunt's voice softly whispering to me. She said, "Cassie, your mom just called and Carrie just passed." I shed a few tears that morning but I had a sense of peace with it. I knew my cousin was in a better place and she was telling me it was going to be okay. The best part of it was, Carrie could smile. Carrie didn't lose her life that night, she gained one, a better one.

Today I want to honor her because she was the reason I chose my path. Maybe her journey on earth was a short one but it had purpose in my life. She was my inspiration to be the woman I am today. She was my start. She is a legacy that I will never forget and I owe it all to her. I decided as I grew older that I wanted to help people like Carrie, so I went down the path of radiology. I wanted to be a Radiation Therapist. That was my plan but God led me another way and I landed on the path of mammography. This shows you, we are not in control. God is.

Where did fitness come into play?

Insanity with Shawn T. Have you ever done this crazy workout program? If you have, you probably know that Insanity is the perfect name for this program because it's definitely insane! My husband and I did these DVDs often. I absolutely loved them, well I hated them too, it was a love/ hate relationship. As I was going to turn off the DVD player something caught my attention on the screen. It said, "Get Insanity certified!" I suddenly found the energy to bring myself to sit up and locked my eyes on the TV and watched. I looked over at my exhausted husband and said, "I want to get certified and instruct these classes." He smiled at me and said," I think you could do it." He could tell the wheels were turning, he knew I wanted to do this.

That evening I lay in bed thinking I want to get this certification. I love this program and I would love to teach it to others. In the back of my mind I thought, "That's stupid, you took public speaking in school and hated it with a passion. Why would this be any different? You can't get up in front of a crowd and teach this. You would freeze with stage fright." Even though I thought all this, I couldn't escape these thoughts burning deep inside my head. I laid there thinking about so many things. I wondered if I could do it. I wanted to, the passion was there but I was scared. I didn't know if I had what it took to do something like that.

I started to think about my childhood and how fitness has always been a part of me and began to remember how fitness started early in my life as a young girl with big dreams. I loved sports. I remember getting home from school and rushing to get my homework done so I would be ready when my dad would pull into the driveway from work. I would rush to get my shoes on, get my glove & ball and meet him outside and ask if he would toss the ball to me.

My Dad would set his lunchbox down and throw the ball up and as he did, it felt like it touched the clouds and as it would come back down I would catch it. This became our routine and I got better and better as time went on. He would toss the ball up again making me run for it and I would chase the ball down and catch it. I loved doing this with my dad, it holds a special memory in my heart.

My Dad was my softball coach and he put me in center field and I wouldn't let any ball get past me. Dad didn't have a lot of time, because he worked a lot, but by just giving in and setting his lunchbox down and giving me the time he did was enough to help me find the gift God was later going to use in my life. My dads passion for sports became mine too. As I grew up I became very passionate about fitness.

As I drifted back from thinking about my childhood. I layed in bed still thinking. I couldn't sleep that night. All these thoughts were running wild through my head. Should I explore this new chapter in my life? Being a fitness instructor was a big decision. I hated being the center of attention and this would make me a focal point to everyone but I had this magnetizing pull towards it. I wanted it but could I do it? Did I have what it took to stand in front of a big group of people and perform? Could I be brave enough? Could I face my fears? I didn't know. All I knew was this thought made me happy but at the same time it scared me to death.

I finally drifted to sleep and when I woke up the next day, I decided to look into this Insanity Certification. I found the information on it and I saw there was a class coming up soon in Pittsburgh. I couldn't believe it. I was so anxious for my husband to get home from work. As he walked into the door after a long day of work, I approached him like a little kid. He sat down at the table and I sat next to him pulling this information up on my phone.

Patrick read the information and he looked at me with those crystal blue eyes and smiled his wonderful smile. He said, "Are you serious? Do you really want to do this?" I locked eyes with him and grabbed his hand and said," I do! I really want to do this!" Patrick said, "Then let's do it!" He is always game for anything. You name it, he is ready. I remember packing our car and heading to Pittsburgh to get my certification. I felt nervous and I kept wondering if I was making the right decision. McGwire was in the backseat and I told him, "We're going to have so much fun." It was Christmas time and I wanted to make this trip worthwhile. McGwire always wanted to go ice skating so I told him we would do that on this trip. McGwire was so excited!

As we drove, I began thinking about my Grandpa John. When my brother and I were little we would spend one week with him in the summer and he would always create an adventure for us. Grandpa was well known and such a big role model to others. I looked up to him, he was my hero. I always told myself I want to be just like him. Every morning before we took off for our adventure, grandpa would bend down to our level and say" WE CAN DO IT" and we would all do a fist bump.This is something I have held my whole life. When I would get scared or about to face something big, I would whisper under my breath "I CAN DO IT" and I would think about my Grandpa.

After daydreaming and thinking about grandpa, I came back to reality. As we got into Pittsburgh my husband was frustrated, I said "What's wrong?" He said, "These roads are confusing me." "I'm lost and the GPS isn't working, I just want to find the closest hotel". We pulled into the first hotel we found. It wasn't the hotel we planned on staying at. My husband was too frustrated to try to find the hotel and the ice skating rank we were planning to go to. McGwire and I were disappointed but we understood. The hotel we ended up staying in was fancy, too fancy for us. There must have been a party because everyone was dressed in tuxedos and beautiful dresses. As we rode up on the elevator with a man in a fancy tux, I smiled at my husband because we were not dressed very nice at all, McGwire had on his superman onesie pajamas and I had on lounge pants and my husband had his jeans tucked into his rocky boots.

As we unpacked everything in our hotel room, I said "We need to make the most of this trip, so let's take a walk." The town was decked out with Christmas lights so we went for a walk, of course we changed our clothes. As we walked through the busy town of Pittsburgh, we heard music and decided to walk towards it. There was a Christmas festival going on and around the corner, there it was, an ice skating rink. My son's eyes lit up and he said "Let's go ice skating!" If that's not the work of God, I don't know what it is. Sometimes we get lost in life and think we aren't on the right path but if you keep walking God will guide you and he will give you something bigger and better. I got my certification that week and the day I stepped in front of my first class, I was terrified. I was so nervous but I remembered what my grandpa used to say to my brother and I. I remembered bumping my hand against my grandpa's rough rugged hand and looking him deep into his watery blue eyes and saying" We can do it." Before I walked out in front of my very first class, I took a deep breath in and I whispered those 4 powerful words, "I can do it."

When Grandpa passed, I felt empty without him. My oldest son McGwire has a vague memory of him but my youngest son Larkin never got the opportunity to meet him. The thing is the memory of my grandpa remains inside of me, he left his legacy with me. It saddens me that my boys didn't get the experience with my grandpa like I did. One thing though, in some ways my boys know my grandpa. They know his qualities, his character, his compassion, his theories and his way of thinking. They know his motivation, his confidence, his beliefs, and his skills because he left his legacy with me.

I carry his legacy inside of me and now I'm passing it to my boys. My boys know him and in some ways met him because they know me and I adopted his character. This is why it is so important to live your life being a good example to those that will be left behind, because they carry on your legacy from generation to generation. My role models in my life formed who I am today. Having good examples in my life built me, structured me, and made me who I am today. They left their legacy in me and I will continue to carry that on to my children so I can leave my legacy too.

When I lost Grandpa it made me think about all the good times with him. We have moments we live in that are so special but instead of living in the moment we find ourselves living in tomorrow. We drift forward into the future and forget that the moment is happening right now. We are always wondering what our future holds for us. Time goes by so fast and when we finally reach the future, we find ourselves living in the past missing those days and wishing they didn't pass us by so fast. We live stressed out and overwhelmed. We wish our days away but then we want them back. We live on repeat.

When we finally sit down and unwind, we look at our kids and see how grown they have become and we wonder where time went. We find ourselves drifting in the past and wanting to go back. We have to learn to slow down and look at where we are right now and enjoy every second of it without having wandering minds. Our minds run so fast, I don't know if we are even listening to each other.

We have to be slow to speak and quick to listen because we are going to miss something special. I hold these memories in my heart of my grandpa taking me and my brother to the park and he would only let us play for a very short period of time. I loved that park and as I played I worried the whole time about when my grandpa was going to say we have to go. I wish I had spent more time appreciating the moment when it was all happening instead of just wondering about when it would end.

These days after losing my grandpa, I just wish I would have enjoyed that moment a little longer. When we are young, we always want to be older and when we are older we're always trying to go back to the time when we were young. We're collecting many little moments. We don't recognize them when we're in them because we're too busy looking forward. But then, as we grow older we spend the rest of our lives looking back, wanting to live those special moments all over again.

My grandpa taught me a good lesson, slow down and enjoy these moments because if we don't live in the moment, we will always be looking back with regret.

# CHAPTER 8

# McGwire Winner

McGwire is the inspiration for me writing this book. He is the reason I get up everyday and flip my laptop open and type. I do it for him, so I can tell his story but I do it for you to give you hope.

When McGwire was little he was a loving and compassionate boy. He had bright blue eyes and always had a smile on his face. He was so sweet and innocent. He wore his heart on his sleeve and he would never hurt a fly. He was such a good listener and never wanted to get into trouble. He told me everything and he was always full of questions.

McGwire was my little sidekick. The bond we had was unbreakable. Wherever I went, McGwire was right behind me. He was my little athlete. He always carried a ball in his hands. It didn't matter if it was a baseball, a football or a basketball, he just always had to play ball, it has always been his passion.

Nothing has really changed about McGwire. He is the same boy, but older. He's thirteen years old and in seventh grade, about to go into 8th grade. I can't believe it. When McGwire was 8 years old, that's when he got sick and that's when everything changed. How did I know? Because he was not the same boy anymore. Everything I mentioned above, when McGwire was sick, everything was the opposite. That's why I knew something was majorly wrong with him. I'm telling you this about McGwire because I believe it's important for you to know who McGwire was before he was sick and I believe it's important for you to know who he is now.

The story I'm about to tell you is going to show you a different side of him. As a Mother, I wanted more than anything to shield him from all this. My intention of writing this book was never to reveal McGwire's weaknesses and to make him look bad. This just goes to show you what a sickness can do to a person. I debated about even writing this. I had this vision years ago to write this book but I kept holding back. I debated over and over whether I should write this book because you will see the nightmare we went through and I didn't want that label on McGwire.

One night, I told him about my vision. I told him I wanted to write a book about him. I also told him my concerns about what people would think about him and he said, "Mom, just do it." I was caught off guard by his reply. I said, "Really," He said, "Yeah, I want you too." "Don't worry about me, I will be fine. People can think what they want, but I want my story heard so we can help other kids like me, or other people that are struggling like I did." He told me that back then he didn't remember a lot of what happened but one thing he knew was everything changed all at once. No one understood what was going on inside of his head and he was scared and he felt alone. He said, "I want everyone to know it doesn't matter how hard things get, there is always a way to fight back but you have to learn how to." He said to me, "Mom, I never knew how to fight back until you taught me how." He said, "Things got better when you taught me about God." "I want you to teach other people about God too." He said, "Nothing is impossible when God is in it, I want people to know that."

This is the reason I am writing this book, because McGwire wants to use his testimony to heal other people and I promised I would do that for him. This book is our family's testimony but McGwire was the one who had to endure the test. He was the one who was sick. He was the one who had to live with the sickness inside him, controlling him. He had to learn to be patient through it all. We all struggle with patience.

Patience is when you have to wait for something to happen. You have to endure it when it hurts. You have to go through the motions when you don't feel like you can move anymore. Patience is not quitting and not giving up. No matter how long it takes, you keep going. McGwire is such an inspiration. He was an amazing little boy before he got sick but he has such a better life now more than he ever has and that's because God is in his life now and it's all because of the struggles he went through.

God only allows these battles in our lives to help us grow. God could easily remove the difficulties from our lives with no problem. God could get you out of the battle faster than he does but the reason he allows it to go on is because he is training us for something bigger. He is equipping us and qualifying us to help people. God is using our battles to help serve Him but we can't do that without the proper training. It's hard to have compassion for people that are struggling when you have never been through anything before. We have to relate to people to understand their pain.

The storm my family has been under was awful and I never want to go through it again, but God restored us. The storm left some scars behind but we use these scars to help heal others. My son is amazing. He has a heart of gold and he helps other kids all the time because he knows what it feels like to hurt inside. McGwire has this magnetizing pull to him that people feel attached to. He has such a positive energy that flows from him that draws people in.

There is a light that shines so bright in McGwire's character. That's what I love so much about him. McGwire knows God. When he has a problem, he now knows Who to turn to. When he gets attacked with harsh words and he feels discouraged, he refers to the word of God. He's now equipped with the proper weapons to help other people fight back. McGwire has a whole new level of understanding of what other people are going through. McGwire is stronger. I have seen this translate into his life in such a powerful way. He's stronger because of his faith in God.

It's confession time, this chapter that you are reading right now, I wrote it a long time ago but I found myself back to writing it again. I was all finished writing this book, so I thought, but I lost this chapter while transferring my book to a different file. Out of all the chapters, I lost McGwire's chapter. The chapter that this book is based around. The chapter that explains the main character of my book. Why this chapter?

I think I lost this chapter because the Devil will always intervene with everything that you start to do that has God in it. He wants to stop you before you do something to help the kingdom of God. I also believe God wouldn't have allowed it to happen unless He had a good reason behind it. Maybe God wanted my last chapter to be about McGwire, maybe He had more for me to add to the story.

I believe God wants you to know that there is a real enemy out there trying to get in your way but don't let him stop you. The Devil doesn't want me writing this book and he sure doesn't want you reading it. Don't listen to him because God knows best and God has the last say in this, not the Devil.

I am currently sitting at the lake rewriting this last chapter. Why at the lake? Well I learned through the years, when God inspires you to do something, you may not be in the most convenient place to do it. I didn't bring my computer to the lake today because, why would I? I have to laugh because I am typing this last chapter on my husband's phone. When God inspires you to do something and even when you don't have everything you need with you, he will supply you with something. You just have to dig deep and find what he equipped you with. God gave me a phone so I am currently using it to type this now.

I am frustrated because I thought I was finished writing this book but here I am back to writing it again. Have you recently lost something that you find yourself fighting to get back? Maybe you are frustrated too. Well then, that's okay, because this book is going to teach you how to fight back for what was stolen from you. If the Devil stepped in and took something from you, don't worry because you will get it back. When you do get it back it will be new and improved. If those dreams feel dead right now, don't trust your fears, because fear is a liar. Stay with me on this path because this journey will bring those dreams back to life with meaning and more purpose.

# CHAPTER 9

# Dreams

What exactly are dreams? First, there are dreams when you have a series of thoughts, images or even emotions as you sleep. I dream a lot and most of the time my dreams don't make much sense at all, and sometimes I can't even remember them. Sometimes they are good, fun dreams and sometimes they're scary, frightening dreams.

I have a dream in particular that I have often. I suppose you would call it a recurring dream. It takes place at a huge carnival, with rides, food, and of course my family is always there. I always feel so good and so happy when I have this dream, and I don't know why because I'm scared to death of rides. I'm adventurous but only when it comes to me being in control. I have no control on a ride, I'm completely vulnerable and I have to rely on some old rusty bolts holding the ride together to keep me alive. Don't get me wrong, I like daring things but I like to do things that I am in complete control of. These rides have all the control, not me and I don't like that.

Another type of dream is the dream that leads you toward your calling. Knowing your skills and strengths helps you to find those dreams. Sometimes you can find a dream through pain and turn pain into purpose. When you have a burning passion inside of you, that is your dream. Usually a dream is something big, it feels bigger than you and a lot of times you don't even think it's possible for you.

Well, this book is going to show you that nothing is impossible with God. What is your dream? I know you have one, we all do, but what is it? Maybe you don't know yet. Maybe the storm you are in right now is making things a little foggy. Maybe the storm is also the one thing that will lead you to your dream. My family's storm led me to mine. God will reveal your true purpose in life in baby steps but sometimes it takes a huge storm to bring it out of you. It also may take a dream, a real, actual, vivid dream to make your calling come to surface. That was my wake up call. Let me ask you this, what if you have a real actual dream that wakes you in the middle of the night and that dream you have changed everything? What if that dream is what brings your dreams alive? Let's explore that thought!

This is how it all started for me. I was getting my kids ready for bed. We went upstairs to their room and I laid down with them to watch some TV until they fell asleep. I remember looking at them and admiring their precious faces as they slept. I gave them both a light kiss on the forehead and whispered mommy loves you as I climbed out of their bed, shut the door and tip-toed down the stairs.

I went down to my bedroom and my husband was fast asleep, snoring away with the remote to the TV still in his hand. I could tell he tried to stay awake while waiting for me, but he didn't make it. I took the remote out of his hand and smiled. I adore that man, he has been so good to me through the years and I'm so thankful for him. I watched a little TV to settle myself down from my crazy day, otherwise my mind would run all night long. When I became sleepy, I shut off the TV and drifted off to sleep.

As I fell into a deep sleep, I had a dream, it was so vivid and so real. In my dream I saw a man in the distance but I couldn't make out who he was. The man in my dream appeared closer and closer, as if he was gliding in the air towards me. As he got closer his face became more detailed and I studied his face. He had mid length, brown shaggy hair with a short brown beard. He had deep chocolate brown eyes and I was captivated and mesmerized by them. I was curious about him, so I studied him carefully. It was as if I was searching for something through his eyes. I noticed his eyes became weak and worried, as if he was concerned about something.

My heart sank into my chest. I became worried too, I felt what he was feeling. I noticed from his left eye a tear developed, it slowly rolled down his left cheek. I remember thinking, don't cry, please don't cry, don't be sad. I didn't know who this man was but I wanted to help him. I wanted to hug him but when I tried to reach my arms out to him, they wouldn't move. I tried to walk towards him but I wasn't getting anywhere. I was stuck. I was fighting but it was as if I was paralyzed.

Anxiety started to rush through me. I looked deeper into his eyes and it was as if he was trying to warn me about something. He slowly started to reach his hand up to me, I wanted to take it but I was awakened from the dream. I rose up out of bed sweating profusely, completely out of breath and my heart was about to pound out of my chest. Fear rushed through me and I began to cry out loud. I looked over at my husband, he was sound asleep and I realized it was just a dream. I laid back down, trying to settle myself. I lay there trying to comprehend my dream, but I didn't understand it. My heart was heavy and my emotions were high. I felt an overwhelming sense of sadness and fear all rolled into one. I got up to use the bathroom and as I returned to bed I thought about my dream some more.

As I closed my eyes to try to go back to sleep, the man's face appeared in my head again. I kept seeing that tear slowly dropping from his face. I tossed and turned trying not to think about it, but I couldn't get his face out of my mind. As I thought about it, I thought, who was that man? I felt like I knew him. He looked so familiar to me. Why was he crying? Why was this dream affecting me so much? I laid there all night thinking more and more about the dream, it was driving me crazy.

Suddenly I rose up out of bed and it hit me right then and there. That man wasn't just an ordinary man, that man was JESUS. My thoughts overwhelmed me. Why did I dream about Jesus? What does this dream mean? Why was He crying? Is Jesus trying to tell me something?

# CHAPTER 10

# Was There More To This Dream?

I have known Jesus since I was a little girl. Well, let me rephrase that, I have known "about" Jesus since I was a little girl. Thanks to my Mom and Dad, I knew who Jesus was. Through this journey, I have learned in the past few years, knowing who Jesus is, is quite different than having a relationship with Him. Growing up, I went to a catholic church and my mom and dad were passionate about God.

My parents made sure my brother and I went to church. We didn't always want to go, we wanted to stay home and sleep in. A lot of times we would pretend we were asleep thinking maybe our parents would forget to get us up and we wouldn't have to go. That never worked, they never forgot, so we went.

I remember my dad saying the blessing every night before dinner and he still does. I also remember before bed, my mom, brother and I prayed every night, but as I got older my prayers stopped and so did church. I didn't carry on that relationship with Jesus that was molded into me. Sure, I prayed to God when times were hard, but I didn't have a true relationship with Him. I would go months without even thinking about God. God only came across my mind when I was struggling with something. Once that was solved, I went on with my life, but God wasn't included.

Having a true relationship with Jesus isn't just talking to Him when you're struggling. I've learned you have to talk to Him on a daily basis. I didn't know that yet, but it makes sense to me now. Just like in life, if I want a good relationship with my husband or kids, I need to talk to them everyday otherwise our relationship will wither away. I know it's hard to talk to someone who is invisible to the eye. We can't see God but He is there and He wants to hear from you. If you start your day with prayer, I promise you will start to see trans-formation in your everyday life. I learned this the hard way, but I'm glad I know this now, because each day is better now when I start my day with Jesus.

Look at it like this. Think of the sunrise. It's so beautiful to wake up and start your day with the sunrise. Whenever my family and I go on vacation to the beach, I will wake up early and slip my shoes on and go for a run on the beach along the ocean. It is so peaceful listening to the waves gently coming in towards my feet. I get lost staring up at the sky as the sun peaks in casting red and orange colors glowing throughout the sky. Everyone at one time or another has marveled over the sunrise.

It is one of those moments that will last a lifetime. There is something special about seeing the first rays of sunlight brightening the sky turning the dark to light. We are naturally attracted to light. Jesus is light. Jesus died on the cross for us but three days later He rose again. He brought back the new meaning of life after death. We might be in the dark at night but tomorrow is a brand new day.

Our dreams may feel dead and hopeless but the day starts over when you wake up to those beautiful rays of sunshine. As you wake up early to watch the sun peak up in the dew of the day, remember this, that the Son rose again, Jesus rose, and you will rise too. Things are not dead, they are alive, there will be joy in the morning. The sunrise is a reminder that it's a brand new day and we can rise again from the darkness and shine our own rays of sunshine. This gives us hope for a better day if the day before was dark. The sunrise uplifts us to a new meaning for a new day. Start your day with the sunrise, start your day with Jesus!

After having that dream of Jesus, I didn't sleep well the next night. I tossed and turned all night long. As the sun peeked through my window, I decided to go ahead and just get up. I couldn't lay there anymore. My dream was heavy on my mind. I made some coffee and went on with my morning routine trying to escape my thoughts, but I couldn't. I sat down in my chair.

I just couldn't stop wondering why Jesus was crying in my dream. I decided to pull up google and I typed in the question, What does it mean when Jesus is crying in your dream? Big mistake, let me tell ya, Google is never the answer. I knew that but I needed some answers, some clarity to this, but I didn't get the answers I wanted. I began reading and it said "Jesus was warning me that I was going to die soon." When I read that, I won't lie, I panicked a little. I kept searching and it got worse. It said, "This is a warning that something is going to happen to a loved one."

When I read that, I freaked out even more. I didn't get the clarity I wanted. I didn't feel better about this at all, I felt even worse. Take my advice, never Google anything, it makes everything ten times worse. I had to get up out of my chair and do something, I couldn't just sit there. I tried to brush it off all morning, but all I wanted to do was cry. I felt stupid that I was crying over a dream, but it felt so real and so detailed. I was scared of what was going to happen. Was I going to die? Or worse yet, was someone in my family going to die?

As my children and husband woke up for the morning, I composed myself and went on with the day. I wanted to do something fun so I could distract myself. I said, "Hey guys it's nice out today, let's go on a picnic." McGwire jumped up and down and was super excited and Larkin knew something was happening so he was excited too. We decided to have our picnic in my favorite place, my backroad, "Paradise." I packed a big lunch for us to take and we all hopped in the side by side and off we went. We rode over the hills enjoying the beautiful scenery the road offered and pulled over to my favorite spot and spread out a blanket and had lunch.

It was such a beautiful day. The wind was perfect, there was a nice gentle breeze, the sun was shining, it wasn't too hot or too cold. I found myself one minute laughing with my family and the next minute my mood would shift and I would feel sad and disconnected from the moment. I would shut down right on the spot and drift away.

Have you ever felt like this? I think we all have experienced this from time to time. Maybe you are dealing with something and trying to avoid it but you find yourself coming back to all the anxiety. You're not alone. This is the work of Satan. He can take such a beautiful moment and corrupt your mind so fast that you crash. One minute you are laughing, the next minute, you are crying. He can manipulate your mind and shift it instantly. The Devil had control over my mind that day. I was in a bad place, I tried to escape it, but I couldn't.

What's ironic about this is, the Devil did this to me in the place I now run to escape those fears. He did this to me where my outlet is, in "Paradise." I have to think that was the beginning of my safe place, of that backroad blessing. I didn't know it yet, I didn't know that this road was my safe place, but Satan did. He will try to take your safe place and destroy it so you never want to go back to it again, but for me, his plan never worked. The enemy may have had my mind that day, but God had my hand.

God brought me to paradise that day for a reason. After we were finished eating, we decided to pack up and head back home. On the way back, I remember looking around at the scenery and it felt good. I had a sense of peace but my anxiety kept taking over. I was having a battle inside. We were almost home and were approaching my mom and dads house. I saw my mom standing outside as we drove by. I asked my husband if we could stop and see mom and dad. He said sure and turned into their driveway. This was an excuse. Really it was me who needed to see her.

My mom is my cushion. When things get real for me and hard to handle, she is my comfort. I may be a grown woman, but there isn't a day I don't need my Mom, she's my lifeline. After we stopped, McGwire jumped out side by side and wrapped his arms around my mom and gave her a great big hug. She grabbed Larkin out side by side and gave him a kiss on the forehead. These boys are her world. When she saw them, her eyes lit up fifty shades brighter.

After she got all her hugs and kisses, she looked at me and gave me a hug and another look. She sensed something was wrong, her radar went off. I couldn't hide my emotions from her. My mom has this special ability to detect that something is wrong with me or my brother, she knows when something isn't quite right with her children, she always has. I also have this instinct in my children too. Call it a superpower, call it what you want, but moms always know.

My mom asked, "Is there something wrong Cass?" That was the question I dreaded to be asked, it was the question that dug deep inside of me. That question always makes me break down and cry. Even though I hated it, deep down it was the question I needed to be asked. I needed to talk to someone about it instead of holding it inside. I needed my Mom to say it's going to be ok, everyone is going to be ok. I let it all out and told her about my dream. I didn't go into detail, but I told her the basics of the dream. I told her about what Google said. I just wanted her opinion on it and what she thought it meant.

She said, "Cass, it's just a dream." "Just because you dreamed about Jesus doesn't mean bad things are going to happen." You can't listen to Google. Dreams are dreams, they don't always reveal things, sometimes we just dream. I wouldn't get real concerned with it, everyone is healthy and everyone will be ok, trust me." That's what I needed to hear, plus a big hug to make it all better. I had to focus on what she said and not what Google said.

When we got home, we settled in for the night. As my husband and I headed to bed I decided to talk to him about my dream. Patrick said, "Cass, I agree with your mom. It was just a dream, everybody will be fine." He always makes me feel better too. There's something about his warm tight hugs that makes me feel better. We watched a little TV and decided to turn it off and go to bed. As my husband drifted off to sleep I lay there staring at the ceiling.

I tossed and turned and the image of Jesus's face was permanently burned into my mind. It got more and more detailed. I was going crazy, I tried to turn it off but it got more and more vivid. I couldn't close my eyes without seeing Jesus' face. I dwelled on that one teardrop slowly rolling down His cheek. I became restless, my heart sank and my chest was heavy. I started to cry, I was sad, and scared. My thoughts overwhelmed me. I didn't want anything to happen to anybody. I started to cry louder.

My husband woke up and noticed me crying. He reached over and rubbed my back. He said," Cass, are you ok? What's wrong?" I couldn't talk but he knew. He asked, "Is it the dream that's bothering you?" I just shook my head yes. He said, "It was just a dream Cass, It's ok." I said, "What if it's not? What if it's a warning? What if something happens to you or the kids? I don't want anything to happen to you guys.'" I cried in his arms and he held me tight until I fell asleep.

Things eventually got better, but in the back of mind I was always on edge preparing myself for the worst. The dream felt so real and it felt like it represented something more. It felt like it had a deeper meaning to it and it felt like it was a warning about something, but what?

# CHAPTER 11

# Changing Paths

As my alarm went off and I dragged myself out of bed and began to get ready for work a sudden gut wrenching feeling hit me. A sense of panic rushed through me. I figured I was just tired, so I hopped into the shower and went on with my usual routine. After I got out of the shower and began to blow dry my hair, the feeling came back, but more intense. Suddenly my chest felt heavy. I tried to ignore it, but I couldn't shake it off. I took in a deep breath and slowly blew it out. I tried to calm myself down but nothing was working.

My husband worked midnights and he always got home just as I was about to leave. Before I left to go to work, I always tiptoed into my kids room and peeked in at them. I never wanted to wake them, so I always blew them a kiss and softly whispered, "Goodbye boys, I love you kiddos." I always hated to leave them but this time it felt different. I had this magnetizing pull towards them. I didn't want to leave, but I knew I had to go. I slipped my shoes on and kissed my husband goodbye and slowly walked to my car. I opened my car door and sat down in the driver's seat and gently laid my head on the steering wheel. I felt sad. I didn't want to leave my boys. I didn't know what came over me. I never felt like this before.

As I started the ignition and pulled out of the driveway, anxiety rushed through me. I had nearly a two hour drive to work and my mind was racing the whole time. I tried distracting myself by listening to music but the further I got away from home, the heavier my chest got. When I finally pulled into the parking lot of my work, I sat there and stared into space. I whispered to myself, get up and go, you can do it. I got out and headed towards the building but I didn't want to walk through those doors, something was pulling me back to my car. I just wanted to go back home and be with my boys.

I wanted to be a mom that day, not a mammographer. I thought this feeling would go away but it went on for weeks. It was getting close to a month and I kept my emotions to myself, but I didn't know how long I could continue going on like this and not talking to my husband about it. I couldn't hide it anymore. I felt like I wanted to quit my job, but just thinking those thoughts scared me. Was I going to just quit and throw my education down the drain? I worked so hard to get where I was. I was happy and content. I loved the people I worked with, they were all my friends.

What was wrong with me? I couldn't quit my job. I needed my job, we would never make it financially on one income. I knew all this and that's why I couldn't bring myself to tell Patrick. I was fighting my emotions. I was in a back and forth battle with myself. Patrick and I needed to have a talk, but when? I knew it had to be soon but I needed the perfect opportunity to do it.

One night after supper, the kids were playing in the living room while I washed the dishes and Patrick dried them. Doing the dishes together was always the time Patrick and I really got to talk about our day. My mind was racing and I knew I was being quiet. Patrick looked over at me and said, "Is something bothering you Cass?" I knew this was the best opportunity to talk to him. I tried to compose myself as I told him how I have been feeling but the tears streamed down my cheeks and I lost it.

I looked back into the living room and saw my kids playing. I said, "Patrick, I've been feeling like I need to quit my job and step away from work for now and be a mom. I want to stay home with our boys and enjoy them. I haven't experienced the joys of being a mother because I'm working all the time. I'm tired of leaving them early in the morning and coming home late at night. It's not enough time with them and I'm going to miss everything and regret it. They're growing so fast. I don't know why this sudden urge has come upon me, but I need to test the waters and if it doesn't work out, I can go back to work."

Patrick stood there and took everything in. I knew I caught him off guard and he didn't know what to say. He put the dish towel down and pulled me tight into his chest and gave me a big hug and looked me straight in the eyes and said, "I've known your heart has always been to stay home with our boys. I want you here with them, I always have. I hate you being on the road all the time. I'm constantly worrying about you. I just wish I had a better job so you could quit. Cass, I don't know if this is going to work. I don't know if we will be able to keep up with our bills."

I began to cry and said "I know, I just don't feel like I can go to work anymore. I don't know why, I can't explain it." I said, "I've been doing my workout classes on the side. I could pick up on those." He started to think about it more, and said, "If this is something that you feel like you really need to do then we can make it work." I couldn't believe he was on board with me. I felt hesitant walking away from my job. I was scared to make this move.

It was risky but my kids were the deciding factor. I said, "Are you sure?" Are we going to be ok doing this?" He said, "It's going to be hard but we're going to make this work." I held my pinky finger up and said, pinky swear. He wrapped his pinky around mine and said, pinky swear. That night we were walking by faith not by sight. We didn't see any good out of this, deep down we were scared we wouldn't make it financially but we sacrificed everything to make our family happy.

The decision we made that night should have never worked. Statistically we should have fallen behind on our bills after I walked away from my job, but somehow we were doing it. From the grace of God, He provided for us. God was preparing us for that sharp turn down a new path that He was about to take us on.

# CHAPTER 12

# Where Do We Go From Here?

A few days later I made the call and quit my job. I was so scared at first. I second guessed myself a few times before I did it, but I thought about my kids and I knew this was the right step to take. A lot of people are under the impression that all encounters with God will come out in a big way but more often than not it's likely God will come out in a small encounter at first.

Taking that step and walking away from my job was an act of faith but it was also my first encounter with God. At the time I didn't know I was walking by faith and I didn't know God was walking with me. I'm a pretty basic person, what you see is what you get. I was now a stay at home mom and I was loving every minute of it. I woke up everyday without a weight on my chest, I felt content and happy.

I was being the mom I always wanted to be. I was finally home with my boys. I could get McGwire off to school and be home with Larkin all day. When that alarm went off everyday, I didn't have the dread that went along with the sound of the alarm. I didn't have to kiss my kids goodbye anymore. I began to instruct more classes and things were going ok at first. Like I said, I'm a basic woman. Our life was ordinary, but God will take the most basic things and put His little spin on it. That's where God works the best, basic. When God uses us, it might start in a small subtle way and you might not realize He is using you.

I was following the path He led me to, but at the time I didn't know God was even leading me. I was walking with no purpose in mind. I was operating under faith without even knowing it. The path God led me to felt good at first, but as time went by, I began having doubts and found myself backpedaling. I wasn't sure if I had made the right choice. At the time I had some people in my life that didn't understand why I walked away from such a good job.

I began to feel like I had no purpose anymore and the guilt started to kick in. Being a stay at home mom is so rewarding and priceless, but yet it is so underappreciated. Maybe you are reading this right now and you're a stay at home mom. If so, this is for you. Never put yourself in a lower status because you're doing more than what you think. Don't listen to other people's opinions, listen to your heart. Being a stay at home mom has its own ministry.

Sure it's a huge decision but yet an important one. Forfeiting a second income is rough, I know the impact it has on a family. Look at what you are doing though. Being home with your children, along with dishes, laundry, dusting, paying bills, going on grocery runs, providing hot meals for your family and driving kids back and forth to school has its own ministry. Instilling values and speaking life into your kids means the world to them. Pouring out advice and listening to them about their day makes them feel heard and gives them hope for the future.

You will never regret providing time with your kids and making memories along the way. Being able to mentor your kids and teach them important morals is meaningful. Making the decision to stay home with your kids is likely the reason your kids will grow up to be something amazing in life because of you and all your structure. Countless times I beat myself up that I gave up on my job but my job wasn't for me. It was the job for me at the time, but I was on a new path and I needed to stay on it. My foundation was laid here at my home.

That all being said, it's also okay to be a working parent too, we all have our ministry. I believe where you're placed in life is where your foundation lies. Your ministry is where you are and sometimes we are placed in some areas for a little while to prepare us for the next chapter of our lives. We need to be content where we are now so it can prepare us for where we are headed. If you can't be content in the small places, how will you ever be able to handle something bigger? God gives us a little and if we learn how to operate with a little, when we least expect it, your little will become a lot.

After quitting my job I constantly juggled back and forth whether I made the right decision. I struggled with not feeling like I was enough, because I didn't feel like I had enough. I had my kids, my husband, and I still had my workout classes. I was the mom that I always wanted to be. Those things felt like something but I wanted my workout classes to pick up more and I wanted my gym to grow, and at first it wasn't growing like I expected.

My gym started in my basement. It was small and I was limited in space. I barely had any equipment, knowledge, or any experience and I definitely didn't have enough people to make a gym. I thought I needed to have a lot of people in my gym to make this transition on my new path possible. Now thinking about it and if God allowed a lot of people in my gym at first, I would have thought it was all those people that carried me through this process and I would have never noticed that this was the work of God.

We can't operate off of feelings, we have to learn to trust the process even if it doesn't feel like enough. As you read this, it doesn't seem like I had enough but my story goes on. Most people in this situation would panic, and I'm here to tell ya, I did, I panicked. My husband never expressed it but I think deep down inside he panicked too. We were struggling financially. My guilt was really setting in. We were struggling and it was my fault. I felt like I should have never quit my job. We had to make some sacrifices since the money was no longer coming in and it was hard at first. Most people in this situation would run back to where they came from and I would be lying when I said that thought didn't cross my mind.

I almost went back to work but my loving husband stopped me because he reminded me of the reason why I left in the first place. I wasn't giving this process enough time to work out. Don't force yourself to go back to something that you know deep down isn't right for you. We can't afford to look back. It's dangerous to tread those rough waters again but we often do this to ourselves because of fear. My advice is to keep walking forward so you don't miss your true calling.

Believe me I wanted to go back, I fought myself day after day. The thought of going back to work cut deep inside me like a knife. I was happy at home with my family but I feared what was going to happen to us financially. I looked way too far into the future. Don't do that, as humans we have the gift to look into the future but what we see most of the time isn't reality. Most likely it's far from the truth and these thoughts are what stops us from finding our true selves. Only God knows your future, so focus on today and don't worry about tomorrow. If God is leading you, trust him and follow him. God knows the true you and He knows what awaits you, He knows you better than you do.

I will be honest, I had a rough start for sure, but one thing I'm going to tell you is that a rough start was my foundation to faith. That rough start was my building blocks. I may have only had a few people in my gym, but those people were my start. Three of them are still training with me today and they play a very important role in my life. They carried me to the next step and because of them being placed on my path they helped me find my purpose.

These people stayed close to me and never left my side. They gave me ideas, opportunities, and a chance, they grew with me. They are part of me, and I would never be where I am today without them. They helped me build my gym and establish it. God placed them on my path for a reason. My dream was there, but these three special people, Angie, Heather, and Kaleb, helped bring my dream alive. They were my beginning to this new path. God always gives you what you need at the time, it may not look like a lot but it's enough to get started. You just have to roll with it and use what you have and that's where faith begins.

Don't focus on what you don't have, focus on what you do have and things will eventually come together. At this time my faith wasn't strong. I didn't even know what faith was. I had lots of doubts and there were times I lost hope. A lot of times I wanted to give up, but faith doesn't mean you're not scared, it's the staying power that builds faith. I had to have courage to keep going. Courage doesn't mean you don't have fear, it just means you are facing your fear. I may have wanted to quit at times, but it's the fact I kept going and didn't give up even when I wanted to due to my faith.

The things I had at the moment felt insignificant, I didn't feel like I had enough of anything but what I had was enough for God to work with. I had to shift my thinking about what I had and not so much what I didn't have. Are you in this position right now? Are you facing something right now that you are backpedaling on? Are you facing regrets? Are you looking back and drifting into the past even though you walked away from it? Did you start something that was burning deep inside your heart but it's not going as expected? Are you wanting to quit, not because of the lack of wanting it, but because of the lack of what you have?

If this is you, it's okay, because this is where I was. My point is, use what you have and God will walk you through it. The most important thing you have is the dream, the vision, you may not have all the things you need to complete the vision but you have enough to get started. For example, what did I have that felt insignificant?

I didn't have equipment but I had some chains, tires, and ropes

I had some ideas

I had a big yard with lots of hills

I had a few people to train

I had a basement

I had a start

I had a dream

I had doubt, but I also had a little faith

These are the things I had that felt so insignificant but in reality, these things were what made me different from other gyms. These things built me and established my mark. I wasn't the same as other gyms, but that's what made me unique. I was diminishing what made me different. I was comparing myself to others. I felt like I wasn't making any progress and all this work was for nothing. I did what I knew and I used what I had, but I felt limited. Your limitations are sometimes what God uses to unlock His power.

In the Bible He constantly used people's limitations to show His glory. When the time is right, God will bring you forth and use you. Maybe you feel weak at the moment but God hides some of our gifts in our weaknesses. The vision you have for yourself may not come alive at first but it builds as your faith grows. With time and patience and with a little faith..

Those chains became barbells

Those tires became dumbbells

Those ropes became treadmills

Those ideas became a class

That yard became my foundation

Those hills became my victory

Those people became my family

My start became my purpose

My dreams were alive and they are still growing

Sometimes just making it by and through a season of uncertainty is all you need. This doesn't mean you aren't scared and you don't second guess it. Most likely you are scared, but some of the biggest things that will happen in your life will be when you are scared. Walking into something that feels bigger than you is scary, but believing that you can do it will carry you through to the next chapter of your life.

A little faith is getting started, big faith is never giving up even when you're scared. My question to you is, what do you have right now to get started? It may not be a lot and it might feel insignificant. My point is, you do have something. What is it that you have? Find it and start with it and see where it takes you. We all have something to start with, and that start is the foundation. It may be a rocky start but if it's a rough road you'll build yourself stronger in the journey of getting there. Sometimes it's not all about the destination you are headed to as much as it's about the journey of getting there and the people you spend it with.

My journey started with some pretty awesome people. We need people in our lives to help us find our way. The people that are placed in your path might be the people that will guide you to the next step. This is for you Angie Vorhies, Heather Gillespie and Kaleb Wilkins. Thank you for believing in me and never giving up on me. You have carried me to this new chapter of my life. I can't thank you enough for sticking with me through this journey!

I would love to end here and say we lived happily ever after but unfortunately this isn't where the story ends. Honestly this is where the journey begins. Life is just like an old back road, you may know those back roads by heart but sometimes we take one too many turns and the road you felt safe on may become dark, foggy, and hard to see. That road will take sudden twists and turns and before you know it you are lost. This is the story of being lost, confused, and scared, but the story will show you what it takes to navigate through the high winds and the torrential downpours of a storm. This is the part where our lives took a sudden turn that was headed to disaster.

I'm going to be honest with you, this is the part of the story I dread to write. Writing about my son and what we went through as a family is so hard. What I'm about to tell you is the part that made me walk away from this book so many times. When I would sit down to write it was like pouring salt into an open wound. Maybe that's because my wounds were never adequately healed. I went through all these years thinking I was healed, but writing this story gave me insight that I was far from it.

Why? I asked myself that often. Why does it still hurt so much? Why can't I write without breaking down and crying? I believe the reason it hurt so much is because I tucked my emotions away for so long and it wasn't until I started writing this book that they started to surface. It caused an overload of emotions I didn't want to deal with. My advice to you is deal with your emotions now, don't do what I did and tuck them all away and pretend you're okay, because more than likely you're not. When I wrote these words, they cut deep inside me and the wounds were still very raw, but God wanted to use the wounds as my testimony.

God is using my scars to show you that I survived, my family survived and you can too. These scars remind me of God's grace. This part of the story isn't fun, but this is the part that's so important because in order to see God's light you have to see the dark path we had to walk down first. Writing this may have been hard but it's for you to see that there's light at the end of the tunnel.

# CHAPTER 13

# The Storm Is On Its Way

I t was a cold December day on a Friday afternoon and it was time for McGwire to be home from school. I loved this moment of the day, I missed him so much and Larkin couldn't wait to see his big brother. Larkin and I were looking out the window as McGwire's bus arrived, and he hopped off. When McGwire walked through the door, he dropped his book bag on the floor and looked up at me and said, "Mommy I don't feel good." I said "oh no" and placed my hand on his forehead and it was hot. I said, "Why don't you lay down on the couch and we'll put some cartoons on and I'll get you something to drink." When I brought him his drink, I took his temperature and it was a low grade temperature.

McGwire drifted off to sleep, he was in and out for a couple hours. When he woke up, he felt somewhat better. I took his temperature again and it was back to normal. The next day he was feeling better and his temperature was still in the normal range. I figured he was tired from a long week of school. Saturdays were my favorite, because my family was home and we were all together and I loved every minute of it. Every year our town has a Christmas festival and this year our local library was going to have an Elf school for the kids. McGwire was so excited about this, he wanted to go so bad. He asked, "Can we go to elf school Mommy?" I bent down to his level and looked into his sparkling blue eyes, and said, "Yes buddy, of course we can."

We arrived in town and walked the streets of McConnelsville enjoying all the beautiful lights that decorated the town. We stopped by some of the local shops and looked around and made our way to the library. As we were walking, McGwire grabbed my hand and looked up at me and said, "Mommy I'm cold." I pulled him close and said "I'll warm you up and gave him a bear hug." I looked at him and said

"We're almost to Elf school!" He smiled real big and was so excited!

As we arrived, we walked into the library and McGwire's eyes lit up! The staff met us at the door, decked out in elf hats and festive Christmas shirts and asked, "Would you like to participate in elf school today?" McGwire shook his head yes and since Larkin was fast asleep in his stroller Patrick decided to walk around with him so I could take McGwire around to see all the fun things to do. As we made our way through the library we saw cookies, hot chocolate and so many goodies to choose from. McGwire grabbed a few cookies and some hot chocolate.

There were several tables set up for the kids to make Christmas decorations. McGwire took my hand and led me to the first table where all the supplies and instructions were available to make your own. He asked me what we were supposed to do. I looked around at the other parents and watched them for a minute to see where they started. I thought to myself, I can do this, right? Yeah, I got this. Ok, so let me give you a little background on my craft abilities, one thing you need to understand is, when it comes to arts and crafts, I'm terrible and that is putting it nicely. I'm not that crafty mom you see on TV. Let me add this too, I'm a high paced kind of person and I don't like to follow instructions, I don't feel like I have the time or the patience. I like to think I can figure it out on my own.

Back to the story. McGwire asked," What do we do mommy?" I picked up a couple of popsicle sticks, some glue, some moving eyeballs, and started creating a masterpiece. I kept watching a dad with his son working on their decoration, and I followed him step by step, but our decoration didn't look anything like theirs. I looked at McGwire and said, "Done, what do you think?" McGwire looked at our decoration and then looked over at all the other kid's decorations and held up the example they made and said, "Mommy ours doesn't look like this." I giggled and whispered, "I know pal, but it's unique, right?" He awkwardly smiled, and said "I guess it is?" I said, "We're just getting warmed up. Let's go to the next station, maybe it will be better."

Nope, it wasn't any better, I think they got worse as we went along. Patrick and Larkin joined us and Larkin was happily eating a cookie with chocolate smeared all over his face. I love my kids all messy like that, they're adorable. McGwire said, "Hey daddy, look at all our decorations" and Patrick burst out laughing, then said, "That's your mom for ya!" I said, "Hey they're one of a kind!" Patrick laughed and said, "Yeah they're definitely one of a kind." This became a big joke and till this day every year we continue to hang those goofy decorations on our tree. As we hang them, McGwire says, "Look mom, here are our unique decorations," and they all start laughing. I say, "Ha, ha, ha, real funny. You will never find a decoration like that!"

That evening when we got home, I tucked my kiddos into bed and later that night, McGwire came down to our room not feeling good. I felt his head and he was burning up. His temperature was very high and he complained of a terrible sore throat. I was concerned, and placed a cold washcloth on his head and gave him some Tylenol, then put him in bed with my husband and I and held him all night. The next morning his temperature was up and down and his throat felt like he was swallowing razor blades. I decided to keep him home from school and take him to the doctor.

When we got there the doctor evaluated him and decided to run a strep test on him. She came back in and said, "Yes, he has strep, it's been going around." It's funny how words will stick in your head for so long, I will never forget the doctor's next words. She said, "It's good you came in when you did, strep can cause a lot of problems, it can get really nasty if you leave it untreated." When she said that, I heard her but I didn't think anything about it.

Those words have stuck with me forever, because she was right, but at the time I didn't know that. At this point I thought we were good to go. We got our antibiotics and were on our way to getting better, so I thought. In reality we were on our way to a nightmare. When we got home McGwire was so tired and drained. He laid down on the couch and I put a blanket in our dryer to warm it up and then covered him up with it.

I learned this method from when I worked as a mammographer. We always provided warm blankets for our patients that were preparing to have a biopsy. We wanted them to be as comfortable as possible as this was a scary time in their lives. I was a biopsy tech and this is what I loved to do as a mammographer, because I was the one who held their hand during the time of uncertainty. I wanted to be the one they could lean on. Maybe God placed me there to prepare me for the moment we were about to face in our lives.

# CHAPTER 14

# Legos

After a few days I saw some improvement in McGwire. His antibiotics were working and his symptoms of fever and sore throat were gone. I could tell he was feeling better because he was up playing with his Legos. I said "Hey, looks like you feeling better?" He looked at me and said, "Yeah I am." I said good and gave him a big hug and asked if I could play. He looked at me hesitantly for some reason and then handed me my Lego character, Cassie Lego. We had many varieties of the Cassie Legos with different hair styles and different outfits.

As I held the Cassie Lego in my hand it reminded me of a memory of our Lego adventures. Legos are so popular these days. There's something special about these little building blocks. McGwire and I used to spend so much time creating our own masterpieces. As you know, I don't use manuals and I'm not much on following instructions. Legos come in a box showing what the objects are supposed to look like and we would try to build them as they were intended to be, but as we worked we would end up creating our own unique objects.

McGwire loved his Legos so much and had such a great imagination. This was his way to create his own little world and we would get lost in it for hours. Legos were our favorite thing to do together. McGwire loved creating his own "invention" as he would call it, and he would tell me how it worked. Legos were our building blocks to his childhood. They carry sentimental value for both of us. I started to drift back and began to remember McGwire's struggle with starting school. He didn't want to go, he didn't want to leave me and I didn't want to leave him. It was hard for both of us. We were best buddies, we were inseparable, but McGwire was growing and we found ourselves in this new chapter of our lives that we both were not ready for.

As I walked McGwire to his classroom, he would turn to me crying, and holding on to me. That was so hard for me because I didn't want to let go of him and leave him knowing he was so upset. He did this every day for weeks. The teacher would always take McGwire's hand and try to distract him and lead him into the classroom. He would always look back at me and I would give him a fake smile so he knew it was okay. I fought my tears as I walked down the long hallways of the school keeping the tears at bay, until I could get to my car where I broke down and cried.

I knew I needed to find a way to comfort McGwire and get him through this. One day McGwire and I pulled into the parking lot of the school. I parked the car and turned to McGwire and said, "Hey bud, are you going to be a big boy today?" His eyes were already tearing up as he nodded his head yes. I said, "You know buddy, mommy will always remain in your heart even if she can't be with you", as I rubbed his little chest. He nodded his head again. I said, "Mommy wants to give you something that will remind you that I am with you". He looked at me puzzled and I said, "Open your hand".

As he opened his little hand, I pulled Cassie Lego out of my pocket and placed it in his hand and then pressed it against his heart. I told him, "When you get sad just hold Cassie Lego and I'll be with you." We got out of the car and made our way down the long hallway and said our goodbyes. He gave me a big hug and pulled his Cassie Lego out of his pocket and said, "I love you Mommy." I blew a kiss to him and said, "I love you too pal" and bent down and whispered in his ear, "Remember, mommy will always be with you." He remained strong as he walked into his classroom calmly and looked back at me one more time and gave me a half smile and I gave one back to him.

As I came back to reality and found myself daydreaming as we were playing Legos, I looked at McGwire and thought he had come a long way. He has grown up so much. He is a big second grader now. We continued to play Legos for a while and then suddenly out of the blue, he said, "I don't want to play Legos anymore." I said, "Okay, that's fine." He looked at me and said, "I feel weird playing Legos." I looked at him in an unusual way and said, "What do you mean by that, pal?"

He got defensive and said, "I don't know, I just feel like I don't like them anymore." I said, "That's strange, you love Legos." He said, "I know but I feel weird playing them."

I didn't understand why he said that and chose to ignore it. I figured he was still fighting the sickness and was tired. I was sure this would pass. A couple of days later. I said, "Hey pal, do you want to play Legos today?" He said "no" in a mean voice and started acting weird about it again. I said, "What's wrong pal, is something bothering you?" He said, "I just feel weird playing Legos. I don't know why, I just don't want to play with them anymore." I wasn't really concerned about this, kids drift back and forth with what they like to play with, so I brushed it off again, no big deal. It wasn't until I started to see more changes in him that I became more concerned about what was going on.

I started to notice a trend of patterns that were not normal for his behavior. McGwire has always been a gentle soul, but things were changing in him and I couldn't quite figure out what was going on. I realized this isn't just about losing interest in Legos, there was more to it, but what? And why all of a sudden?

# CHAPTER 15

# The Changes Were Coming

A s time passed by things got progressively worse. I started to be more in tune with McGwire and was trying to figure out what was going on with him. We were on Christmas break from school so I was able to evaluate him a little more. I began to observe things I never saw in him before. As I studied him, I discovered he was developing OCD tendencies.

He was constantly washing his hands all day long. I would say, "McGwire you just washed your hands" and he would say, "I can't get them clean, they're still dirty. I keep touching dirty stuff." I said, "That's a good thing to do pal, but you don't have to wash them all the time, they'll be fine." I started to notice he was becoming sensory sensitive. His eyes were very sensitive to the light. Bright lights really started to bother him. He was constantly wanting to sit in a dark room. When I would flip the lights on he would yell at me telling me to turn the lights off, while he squinted his eyes to try to block out the light. I told him, "It's dark in here and we don't want to sit in the dark room do we?" He said, "I do, the light hurts my eyes."

I noticed noises were bothering him too. If anything was too loud he would cover his ears. He didn't like Larkins noisy baby toys, he would yell at Larkin to turn them off. The noises never bothered him before but now they had become very annoying to him.

He was also developing hypersensitivity to his clothing. Anything with a seam in his clothing would irritate him. He refused to wear certain textures like jeans or socks with seams in them. His underwear was his biggest problem. He was constantly tugging on them and fidgeting. He would get mad and would say he needed new underwear. When I bought him new underwear, it was always the same thing.

All of this was coming on so sudden and I didn't know why. I started to research OCD. McGwire's symptoms matched it to a tee. I didn't know what to do. Maybe it was a stage he was going through? I had a lot of thoughts running through my head, I just knew this wasn't my boy.

# CHAPTER 16

# Christmas Cookies

McGwire continued to show signs of OCD, but I wasn't sure if maybe it was something that would pass. Or maybe it was something I could help him with because I had some OCD tendencies myself. I always strived to be perfect at everything I did. I needed everything to be organized and placed in a certain spot and everything had to be clean. I was cautious with hand washing and with germs, not in an obsessive way but it was always in the back of my mind. Maybe this is what he is going through.

My dad has the same OCD tendencies. If I went to his garage and moved one of his tools, he would know it. My dad has always been very particular with his garage. It is immaculate. I started to convince myself this is all normal, it runs in the family. I could get him past this with a little work. He's 8 years old and at this age he's growing and developing his own thoughts and feelings. At this age, he's trying to figure himself out and he's going to test the waters.

I figured this is very minor. Something I could help him overcome. I felt confident about this until I started working with him and it began to backfire on me. He began to get very angry with me as I worked with him through this. I noticed he was starting to distance himself from me. All I wanted to do was help, but all he wanted to do was push me away.

I started to see a trend of him wanting to hide all the time. He was always in a closet or cubby hole hiding. I wasn't sure what that was all about. There were so many things happening all at once and I couldn't absorb it all. I wanted to backpedal and start all over again. I was trying so hard to help him but maybe it was out of my hands and I needed professional help. I started to realize this was more serious than I thought. I needed my mom and her opinion.

I told my mom everything and she said, "I will come over and we can make Christmas cookies and I'll evaluate him." My mom and I have been making Christmas cookies together for years and we have carried on the tradition with my boys. Every year we get together and put on some Christmas music and start baking. The boys love it! Things had been chaotic with McGwire and I thought this is just what we needed. Maybe this would get him out of the slump he was in. My mom called and said she was going to come over and wanted me to get the boys ready so we could start baking.

That morning I walked into the living room to tell the boys to get ready for Meme to come over so we can start making Christmas cookies. Suddenly I noticed Larkin was sitting in the living room playing with his toys but McGwire was nowhere to be found. I walked around the house calling his name but didn't get an answer. Finally I heard an eerie laugh coming from the closet. I knew at this point he was hiding from me so I went with it. I said, "McGwire where are you?" Then he laughed that eerie laugh again. Then I popped into the closet to scare him and he started running away and hid again. I said, "Are we playing hide and seek?" I smiled and he took off running and laughing again.

That laugh was so weird. It reminded me of the Joker from Batman. I said, "Bud, we can play hide and seek later, we have to get ready to make cookies, Meme is on her way over." I looked around for him, playing his game and found him again. He started running again and I said, "McGwire we have to get ready bud" he said, "No, I'm hiding" and his face got very serious and he hid again.

Then we heard a knock on the door and Mom let herself in. Larkin met her at the door and she picked him up and asked, "Are you ready to make Christmas cookies?" She then asked where McGwire was and I said, "I don't know where he is," very loudly, then whispered, "He's hiding." She nodded her head and started walking around the house looking for him saying, "McGwire where are you?" When she finally found him, he laughed that weird laugh again. Mom looked at me in a strange way and I said, "I don't know, that laugh is new to me too. It's probably something he picked up at school." Finally we got McGwire and Larkin ready to make cookies.

This year felt different. Something was off with McGwire. He wasn't his usual bubbly self. As we prepared to make cookies McGwire's focus wasn't there. It was as if he didn't want to be there. He barely cut any cookies out and putting the frosting on usually was his favorite part but it was as if I was forcing him to do it. All he wanted to do was hide. He kept sneaking off and hiding. When I would go find him again, I would try to refocus him to sit down and put the frosting on the cookies but he would get mad at me and lay his head down on the table.

This year was feeling hard and it didn't feel how Christmas usually felt. McGwire was my kid that loved Christmas so much, but this year he didn't seem to be into it. I didn't know if it was his age and he was losing interest in Christmas or if it was something else, something deeper. I couldn't put my finger on it. When we got everything cleaned up and mom was about to leave, McGwire started crying. He said, "I don't want Meme to leave, I want to go to Meme's house."

This wasn't unusual, the kids loved their Meme but his behavior was different. He started screaming, not wanting her to leave. I tried to hug him and tell him it was okay and that he would see Meme tomorrow, he pushed me away and hugged her. Mom said, "He can come over for a little bit, so I didn't fight it and I allowed him to go. I figured after a couple hours at her house, he would be ready to come home. As a few hours passed I called to see if he was ready to come back but he had a meltdown. He said he wanted to stay all night with her and I allowed him to do so. I figured he needed a night with his Meme.

The next day when I went to Mom's house to pick him up, he had another meltdown throwing himself to the ground. He didn't want to leave and he fought me. I said, "Pal, we have to go." I have some Christmas activities to do with you and Larkin. He said, "I don't want to do them with you, I want to stay here with Meme. I felt sad.

McGwire always wanted to do all the fun Christmas activities but this year he didn't want anything to do with them. He started to become very attached to my mom and became more distant from me. The next couple days I noticed McGwire was very defensive towards me and defiant. Everything I said to him, he would twist and turn it and it would end up in a big fight. McGwire and I rarely had problems, sure he's a kid and he has had his moments but not like this. His behavior started to really decline.

My sweet boy was becoming very mean. I was losing connection with him and he was pushing me further away and pulling my mom deeper in. Two weeks ago, it wasn't like this, why all of a sudden? Christmas wasn't bright and joyful like it usually was, it was becoming dark. This was all happening so fast and I couldn't comprehend it all.

As a few days passed McGwire grew very cold with me and the hugs began to stop and the distance between our mother and son relationship began to grow further apart. I didn't know what I did to deserve all this. I found myself always trying to get through to him but he was always pushing me away for some reason and I didn't understand it. All I knew was I needed to find out what we were dealing with and why it was happening. It was a week before Christmas and I was so empty inside. Honestly I just wanted Christmas to be over.

# CHAPTER 17

# Nightmares

E ach day we were getting closer to Christmas but the magic wasn't in the air. McGwire's behavior was declining and his OCD symptoms were getting worse. This was coming on so fast. I wasn't prepared for any of this. I was exhausted and drained. I couldn't sleep at night because I was so worried about McGwire. When I woke up I began to have anxiety knowing that I had to fight through another day.

I didn't know what I was going to do. The days were so exhausting because Mcgiwire was constantly pushing me away and I was using so much energy to try pulling myself back in. It became a fight trying to figure out how to help him through this. This was a matter of two weeks that this all came on, but it felt like a lifetime.

McGwire started to develop unpleasant compulsive thoughts. He was constantly going around the house checking the doors to see if they were locked. He feared someone was going to break in. I would reassure him that the doors were all locked and no one was going to break in. It became a fight trying to get him to bed. Just getting him to go upstairs was a real battle. My husband would have to carry him up while he was kicking and screaming.

When McGwire would close his eyes he saw visions of scary creatures that I couldn't wrap my head around. He would scream, haunted by his thoughts. He wouldn't let me hold him or reassure him it would be ok but he needed me there to protect him from the visions. He was caught up between two barriers of pushing me away but yet pulling me in so I could protect him. The only way he would let me help him was by distracting his thoughts by telling him peaceful stories that would calm his mind until he would fall asleep.

This sometimes took hours because he fought the battle inside his head all night long. McGwire was in another world, a world I didn't understand, a world that a little boy shouldn't have been exposed to, but one I wanted to rescue him from. My stories were the only way I could do that. I didn't understand where these thoughts came from. He never watched scary movies or anything that would give him these thoughts. I didn't understand any of this.

Why wouldn't he let me hug him anymore? He loved to cuddle and hug but he didn't want me to do any of that anymore. He always loved our bedtime routine. We would stretch out in bed and watch movies but he didn't even want to do that anymore. We tried watching the Grinch, it was his favorite Christmas movie. When I turned it on, he screamed and said the grinch was too scary and he began visualizing the grinch as one of the scary monsters in his head. He was scared of absolutely everything. Things he was never scared of before. After a long night of telling McGwire stories, I would be so exhausted that I found myself struggling to sleep. I would just lay there and cry.

This went on for days. Was this how it was always going to be? Was this our life now? I knew we couldn't go on like this forever, I needed to get to the bottom of this. I needed to get him help. I felt as if I was failing as a mother. One night after McGwire fell asleep, I found myself lying there beside him watching him while he slept. I felt so bad for him, I hated that he had to fight this and I didn't know how to help him. I missed him, I missed his smiles, I missed his giggles, everything seemed like it was gone in an instant.

I just wanted to hold him but he wouldn't let me hold him anymore. I wanted in, I wanted to at least give him a hug and say it's going to be ok. The thing was, I didn't know if it was going to be ok. As I layed there beside him after a long night of telling him stories I watched him breathe and I began rubbing his cheek and I kissed his forehead and whispered, "It's going to be ok, we're going to figure this out."

I took this opportunity to draw him close and wrap my arms around him and tell him "I love you." I sobbed so hard because this was the only opportunity I had to hold him. A lot of times I would stay there and sleep in his bed all night because I never wanted to let go of him, I needed to hold him in my arms. I needed to take in this tender moment of being able to love him like I wanted to because I knew when he woke up I would have to face another day of him being cold. I desperately wanted my bright blue eyed boy back.

I couldn't take it anymore, I needed answers now. I laid there all night awake, thinking about everything, about the change, it happened so fast and now I was suddenly laying there scared of what was happening. A couple weeks ago, everything was normal and happy, what happened? Now I was laying there in distress and pain. My son was different and he was just as confused as I was. I didn't know how to help him, I was lost. He was struggling and hurting so bad inside and I didn't know why. I needed to figure this out.

Finally I said, enough! I folded my hands together and I started to speak in a whisper, I said, "God, it's me, Cassie. I know it's been a while but I really need you right now, McGwire needs you. We need your help. My son is sick. I don't know what's wrong with him. I don't understand what is happening to him but we need answers." With tears rolling down my face, I said, "God I don't know what to do, please help. Amen."

# CHAPTER 18

# Christmas

I t was Christmas Eve. I loved the magic of Christmas Eve, the anticipation of Santa coming, I loved everything about it. Christmas Eve this year wasn't the same as it usually was but we tried to make the most of it. I tucked the kids into bed that night and McGwire had a little excitement about it being Christmas Eve so I felt some relief to see him happy. I still had to fight with him to go to bed and tell him stories, but he settled because of the anticipation of Santa coming. I went to bed feeling better about everything.

As I fell asleep, I was suddenly awakened by McGwire. He came down to my room around 3:00 am and he had an upset stomach. All night long he kept running to the bathroom. He couldn't sleep, he kept asking me, "Can we get up and open presents." I told him, "Not yet bud, we have to wait for Larkin to get up, try to get some sleep pal" This went on all night. He continued to run to the bathroom and he kept asking me if we could open presents and I would always answer him the same way.

It began to be a repetitive process and the question started to feel more like a demand. As the night went on he went back and forth to the bathroom, and asked the same question over and over. The sun was coming up and McGwire jumped out of bed and said, "It's time to open presents!" I got Larkin up and the boys unwrapped their presents.

McGwire opened his presents as fast as he could and he would throw them off to the side and go on to the next. I told him, "slow down, I wanted to see what he got." He would look up at me and say," I didn't get anything good." I said, "What do you mean, you wanted all these presents." He said, "I don't like any of them." He ran over to the couch and laid down. I went over to him and said, "Don't you want to play with some of your presents?" He said, "No, I hate them." I said to him, "That isn't very nice. Why are you acting like this?" He got up and ran up the stairs to his room.

I ran upstairs after him and said, "Hey bud, I think there's a surprise in the basement." He said, "Ok, fine." He slowly walked down to the basement to see the surprise. It was a blue four wheeler. The four wheeler was what he wanted the most for Christmas. He has been dreaming of getting a four wheeler for a couple years and finally he got it. When he saw it he looked at me and said, "I don't want a four wheeler anymore, I will never ride it." He started to cry and said, "I'm scared of it! I might fall off of it and get hurt." I was dumbfounded, completely blown away, I couldn't believe it. He was never afraid of anything like that. He was always fearless.

He started to run up the stairs and I grabbed his hand to try to stop him and give him a hug but he aggressively shook his hand out of mine and ran up the stairs. I looked at Patrick with tears in my eyes and said, "What is wrong with him?" I was scared. McGwire loved Christmas so much and when he would open presents he would smile the whole time and would want to play with them right away. Not to mention the four wheeler, he would have been on it ready to ride. I ran up the stairs. McGwire was nowhere to be found.

I looked around and I couldn't find him. I realized he was probably hiding, this became his new norm. I found him hiding in a closet. I stooped down and asked, "What's up bud, why are you so unhappy?" He shrugged his shoulders and started crying. He asked, "When is Meme going to be here?" I said, "Soon." A few minutes later we heard the front door open and my mom and dad came in all jolly saying, "Merry Christmas!" To their surprise no one was happy.

McGwire walked over to my mom and gave her a big hug and she said, "Merry Christmas, what did Santa bring you?" He said, "Nothing good." She looked at me and then back at him and said, "What do you mean, it looks like you got a lot of great presents!" He said, "No, I don't like them. I want to go to your house, Meme." She said, "No, we're going to eat breakfast here." Every year we would take him to the football field and play football. He loved it so much, it became his favorite tradition. Two weeks before he was talking about how he couldn't wait to go to the football field and do our family tradition. I thought this would spark some interest in him and change his attitude. I thought he just needed to get out and get some fresh air.

I said "Let's go to the football field and play some football, Larkin is going to stay with Meme and we can head on down!" He said, "I don't want to, I want to stay with Meme." I said, "What, you love football! Look outside, it's snowing and it will be so much fun". He said, "Fine, we can go." The car ride to the football field was very quiet. He sat in the backseat looking out the window. I looked back at him, and felt sad because he looked so unhappy. Usually we would be singing Christmas songs and enjoying the day but not this time. When we pulled into the football field, I got out of the truck and grabbed the football.

McGwire slowly got out and just stood there. At this point big flakes of snow were falling and it was coming down harder. I said, "McGwire, look at the snow, it's beautiful." He just looked at me and said nothing. I threw the football towards him and said "catch", but he just stood there and let the football hit him and said, "I don't want to play, I don't really like football anymore." I said, "Buddy, football is your favorite sport. You have loved it since you could walk." He said, "I just don't like it anymore, I don't know why. Can we leave? I want to go see Meme."

This was so unusual, McGwire loved everything about football. Normally he would be running around the field never wanting to leave, not this year. I decided to try something else to bring him out of this mood. I threw a snowball at him and he just stood there and let it hit him. He had no expression on his face. He just sat down and stared into space. I sat down beside him and he scooted away from me and I asked him, "What's wrong pal?" He said aggressively. "I told you, I don't know, quit asking me."

This was not like him to talk to me like that. I was really upset, and walked away and began to cry. It was Christmas day, out of all days, McGwire acted like he hated everything, including me. Patrick came over and hugged me and said, "Cass it's ok, I don't know what got into him, but we'll figure this out." I said, "let's just go home.

There's no point in us wasting our time if he doesn't want to be here."
When we got back, my mom saw us come to the door and said, "That
was a quick game. Did you guys have fun?" McGwire said, "no" and I
began to cry again. He sat down on the couch and I attempted to sit
beside him but he looked at me and said, "I don't want you sitting by
me."

That hurt when he said that but I took it. I was getting used to him
talking to me that way. I said, "Well I'm going to, whether you like it
or not." I handed him one of his handheld video games he wanted for
Christmas and said, "let's try playing this," He said, "I don't want to,
it's stupid." I couldn't take it anymore, I had held it in long enough.
I instantly got mad. I said, "McGwire, you should appreciate all
these presents you got for Christmas. "This is not how you should be
acting." He got mad and looked me in the eyes and began to cry and
said, "I hate you" then got up and ran to his room.

That hit me like a ton of bricks. I began to cry uncontrollably. My
mom came in and gave me a big hug and said, "What is going on with
him?" I couldn't talk, I just shook my head. My husband was angry
that he spoke to me that way. Patrick started to head upstairs after
McGwire but I stopped him and said, "Just let him go. Something is
wrong with him. This isn't him. He's fighting something." That night
when I tucked the boys into bed, McGwire didn't want me to lay with
him, he was very distant. He needed his story but he didn't need me.
My heart was broken, he was lost and so was I.

# CHAPTER 19

# I've Reached My Breaking Point

The next day after Christmas I had hoped McGwire would wake up and be himself again. That he would come running down the stairs like he used to, but when he came down that morning it was the same. Day after day he became colder and more distant. He continued to cry wanting to go to my moms and sometimes I let him and sometimes I didn't. It was easier to let him go because I didn't have the fight, but I didn't give up.

I wasn't taking the easy way out. I was his mom and I was going to fight for him and solve this. I needed him here even if it hurt me to see him in this condition. I really got concerned when he started complaining about terrible headaches at the top of his head. He would hold his head while laying on the couch crying for me to take the pain away.

I gave him Tylenol but it didn't really touch the pain. I knew McGwire was developing inflammation all through his body. One day he was limping and I asked him, "What did you do to your leg?" He said, "I don't know what I did, but my ankle hurts." Next it would be his wrist, then his knee, or his elbow, the list goes on. It got to the point his joints ached all the time. It seemed as though his whole body was being attacked. I wasn't sure what was going on with him.

McGwire was very active but I saw his activity level decrease substantially. He was constantly laying around watching TV. If you knew him, he was full of energy and was always running around playing, but I wasn't seeing that anymore. I noticed he was watching baby shows instead of the Ninja Turtles, Power Rangers, and Avengers because they were now scary to him. He refused to watch them anymore. He was scared of things that really weren't scary but in his mind they were. It was as if everything he once loved became things he couldn't stand anymore.

McGwire loved Nerf gun battles so I decided I would start a Nerf gun battle and as I did, he gave me a mean look and said "Stop, I don't want to play." I couldn't believe it. As you know, Legos were always our thing. One day I handed him his Lego character and grabbed mine and said "Let's play." But as soon as we started, he looked at me and said "I don't want to play. Remember, I don't like Legos anymore." I said, "What is going on with you?" He threw down the Lego and said aggressively, "Nothing, I just don't like that baby stuff anymore."

McGwire started developing an attitude. He began talking mean to me all the time, then jealousy kicked in. He told me I liked Larkin more than him. I told him I loved him and his brother the same. When I tried to hug him he would push me away and say, "No, you don't want to hug me, you don't love me, you love Larkin." I told him, "Yes, I do love you McGwire." He began distancing himself from me more and more. I found myself going through stages. One minute I would shower him with kindness trying to get him back to himself and other times I was irritated with him and my mothering instinct would kick in and I would discipline him. I didn't want him to be disrespectful.

The problem I found with discipline was, he had a lot of insecurities and when we disciplined him, his insecurities got worse. He took things the wrong way and it caused him to cry. This would send him into a panic attack. He screamed he couldn't breathe and gasped for air and I did everything to calm him down. After having episodes like this, I was scared to discipline him. Panic attacks started happening on a regular basis, it didn't take much to set him off. So we had to be careful what we said to him. We found ourselves walking on eggshells.

Our days became long and agonizing and our evenings took a turn for the worse. One evening McGwire was at my moms house and I wanted him to come home. It was a fight and a real struggle to get him home whenever he went over there. We had to listen to him cry and throw a fit but I needed him home. He was my son and I was his Mother, and even if it meant he was going to be cold and hard, I had to take it because I needed to be with him. When we finally got him home, I decided to try to do something fun with him. He always loved to play tag so I decided we should do it as a family, like old times. Maybe he would play and remember the fun we used to have. I was willing to do anything to get him back.

McGwire went to the bathroom and as I saw him walking out, I tagged him and said, "Tag you're it" and started running. He hesitated for a second but suddenly he started playing. He began chasing us. I was so happy, finally my family was smiling. My son was coming back. As we ran around the house I started thinking about the times of playing tag, chasing him and wrapping my arms around him for a big bear hug then turning it into a tickle fight. I remembered looking into his big blue eyes as I tickled him and seeing his big smile. He would say, "I love you so much mommy!" I would say, "I love you more" and he would say, "No you don't, I love you more." I would blow him a kiss and he would pretend to catch it and put it in his heart and he would blow me a kiss and I would also pretend to catch it and put it in my heart.

This memory was so special but as I ran around chasing him, tears were dripping down my face. I wanted my son back so bad. He hasn't said he loved me for such a long time. My emotions were consuming me. I was happy because we were playing tag but I was sad because I didn't know how long it would last. Suddenly McGwire began to shut down, he slowed down and began to walk away. I had to keep the game going. I couldn't lose this moment so I tagged him again and said, "You can't get me." As I said that I noticed his face changed, it became mean. I slowed down and then unexpectedly, he tackled me to the ground and was on top of me.

Everything felt as if it was in slow motion. I just layed there and studied his face and I saw fear and sadness in his eyes. His eyes flooded with tears, and he began hitting the floor one punch after another, harder and harder, then faster and faster. He was angry but I could tell his anger was masked with fear. He was fighting something deep inside of him. I sat up and tried to wrap my arms around him to stop him and to give him a hug to calm him down. He began pushing his way out of my hug.

Patrick came running over realizing what had happened and he picked McGwire up off of me and McGwire tried to fight his way out of Patrick's arms as Patrick was trying to carry him to the living room. Patrick sat him down on the couch and said, "You need to calm down." McGwire stood up and dropped to the ground as if he didn't have the strength to stand. He went into a full blown panic attack.

I ran to him and he was in the fetal position yelling," I can't breathe, something is wrong with me, help me!" He was sobbing as he said, "I can't help what I'm doing, I can't control it, I'm scared Mommy. I didn't mean to tackle you." He let me hold his hands and I looked him in the eyes, and said as I cried, "It's ok, I know something is wrong with you. You're going to be ok. Just breathe pal. Take a deep breath in then blow it out, slow your breathing down for Mommy. He listened to my instructions and he started to calm down.

He sat on the edge of the couch and said, "Why is all this happening to me? What's wrong with me?" A tear began to roll down his face, I wiped it away and said," I don't know pal, but we're going to figure this out. We will get to the bottom of this but you need to see a doctor, ok?" He hated going to the doctor, but this time he agreed.

He finally realized something was wrong with him. That night he was crying out for help, he didn't have the energy to fight it anymore. He finally broke, but sometimes you have to break before you get put back together. McGwire was trapped and I had to step up and try to figure this out and help him, but how? So I did what I always do when I need help, I called my Mom.

# CHAPTER 20

# We Figured It Out

T hat night I fought getting McGwire to bed. I had to do my normal storytelling to get him to go to sleep. Patrick had to work that evening so I was alone and was scared for my son. It was late but I decided to call my mom. I just needed to hear her voice. When she answered, I broke into an uncontrollable cry, I couldn't help it. I stayed strong for McGwire that night but when I heard my moms voice I knew I could let go and let it all out. I knew this would startle her to answer the phone to hear me crying, but I couldn't help it.

When she heard me, she automatically was worried and said, "What's wrong Cassie?" She was always on the edge of her seat with all this, because lately she got a lot of phone calls from me when I was crying, it became the new norm. After explaining everything to her, she asked me, "Do you need me to come over?" I said "Yes mom, I need you." I was hoping she would ask because I did need her. My mom would never let me fight something like this without her. She would walk through fire for me and at this time she was doing just that. She is such a great mom and I have been so blessed to have her as my mother.

I impatiently watched out the window anticipating her arrival. As I saw her car lights shine into my living room window, I met her at the door. I quietly opened the door so we didn't wake up the boys. I could tell she had been crying and when she walked in, she studied my face and saw I was a mess and gave me a big hug and said her four famous words, "This too shall pass." My whole life, my Mom would always use this bible verse and it would make me feel better. She looked at me and said it again, "Cassie, this too shall pass but you need to hand this over to God, do you hear me?" I couldn't talk, I just nodded my head yes.

We settled ourselves down and mom told me a funny story to lighten our moods. I needed a little laugh to get me through the evening. Mom knows me so well and she knows how to calm me. Mom got serious again and said, "Ok, Cassie, what do you think is going on with him?" I said, "I thought at first it was just his age and he was getting mouthy.

Then I explored down the road that maybe he was jealous of his little brother. I thought it was a stage he was going through that might pass, but there's no getting past this. He's getting worse. Everyday his anger for me grows and everynight the images in his head get scarier. I thought he had OCD but he has a lot of other issues that don't completely go along with OCD. I don't know what's wrong but I do know he was fighting something tonight that shows me he doesn't feel right and he's scared. I thought he hated me and sometimes it still feels that way but I don't think he's fighting me. He's fighting something else and because of that, it's causing him to push me away. He showed me that tonight. I need to get him some help. I need to fight for him, but how? I don't know what to do. This is deeper than jealousy."

She said, "I know Cass." She placed her hand on mine, and said, "We'll figure it out. Can you think of anything this could be coming from? Has something happened to him recently that could be causing all this?" I started thinking, I haven't had time to absorb all this. I thought deeper, then suddenly I said out loud, "Strep!" She said "What?" I said, "McGwire had strep throat!" She said, "Yes he did but he was on an antibiotic for that and it all cleared up, right?" I said, "Yes, but I remember the doctor said it's a good thing we came in when we did because strep can cause some nasty things to happen."

My mom asked, "What kind of nasty things did she say?" I said, "I didn't ask because I thought we were ok. I thought we got McGwire to the doctor fast enough and caught it before those things happened, but maybe not. What if the antibiotic wasn't enough? What if he still has strep?"

Mom grabbed her phone and looked up what kind of harm can happen if strep isn't completely gone out of someone's system? She started reading, and I could tell she was deep into reading it. I asked her what she found. She said, "What kind of symptoms is he having?"

I said, "Well, his personality has changed, he doesn't have much interest in anything, he's attached to you and is pushing me away. He has joint pain all the time and it all happened within the last few weeks. Why? What did you find?"

She said, "Well it says here, if strep isn't completely treated it could cause something called PANDAS." I said, "What? " Mom said, "PANDAS!". I said, "Like the bear?" She said, "Yes!" I said, "What are the symptoms of PANDAS?" My mom looked at me with tears in her eyes. She said, "Cassie, I think we are dealing with PANDAS." My heart sank. "What is Pandas?"

# CHAPTER 21

# PANDAS

What exactly is PANDAS? PANDAS stands for Pediatric Autoimmune Neuropsychiatric Disorder Associated with Streptococcal infections. Strep throat is a very common childhood illness. Some kids get it over and over and a simple round of antibiotics will clear it up. In some cases, a very small number of children, the infection will trigger strange behavioral changes.

What happens is, it causes inflammation in an area of the brain called basal ganglia, which helps govern emotions and motor control. With PANDAS it may seem like the child changes and turns into a different person overnight. The symptoms are usually dramatic and out of the blue and can include motor or vocal tics or both and obsessions and compulsions or both.

In addition to these symptoms children may become moody or irritable. They may experience anxiety and/ or panic attacks. They may show concerns with separating from a certain person and detaching from other people. Strep can hide out in other parts of the body.

The infection will attack the body instead of the germ. It can bring on sudden symptoms such as OCD, sensory issues, sleep disturbance, urinary frequency, joint pain, fears, temper tantrums, baby talk, trouble focusing or paying attention, crying and laughing at inappropriate times, seeing and hearing things that are not there, obsessive thoughts, depression and anxiety. PANDAS can be misdiagnosed as OCD.

PANDAS is a very understudied disease and a lot of doctors are not familiar with it or how to treat it. Doctors are not sure what causes PANDAS and why some kids get it and others don't. Doctors believe

PANDAS appears to be an autoimmune disorder. This is when an infection causes your immune system to attack your body's healthy cells, in this case, cells in the brain.

# CHAPTER 22

# The Doctor's Office

I couldn't sleep that night. Mom and I spent most of the night researching PANDAS and it scared me. It was so new and so understudied but there was no doubt about it, I knew that McGwire had it but I didn't know much about it and what road we were headed down. All I knew was that this was happening whether I liked it or not, this was real. My son was sick. In one way I was reassured that we figured out what was possibly going on with him. In other ways I didn't want this to be the answer because it didn't sound good and I was so afraid.

I layed there on my couch trying to go to sleep but I couldn't, my mind was racing and I could only think about all the worst case scenarios. I could only imagine the torment my son was going through. This hurt me so bad because as a mother I wanted to take this from him and help him but I couldn't. Mom laid on the other end of the couch. I knew she wasn't asleep either. I said, "Mom, I'm scared." She said, "I know you are, but it's going to be ok Cass. We'll go to the doctors first thing in the morning. You need to get some sleep, it's going to be a long day tomorrow." It opened at 8am, I wanted to be early so we could get to the bottom of this as soon as possible.

I drifted to sleep but as fast as I fell asleep I was awakened by the sun peaking through my living room window. My husband got home from work and we explained everything to him. I heard footsteps through the kitchen heading our way and McGwire walked into the living room and he noticed my mom sitting on the couch. He was puzzled. He asked, "Why are you here Meme?" I said. "She stayed here last night." He said, "She did? Can I go to your house, Meme?"

My mom said, "Not today buddy." She took his hand and said,

"We're going to go to the doctor today." He pulled his hand out of hers and aggressively asked, "Why?" My mom exclaimed, "You haven't been feeling good and we want to help make you feel better." He said, "I feel fine. I don't want to go to the doctor." I said, "Buddy you know you don't feel right, you said so last night." He was mad and said, "I lied, I feel fine." My mom said, "Let's get ready buddy." McGwire took off running to his usual hiding spot in the kitchen. A while ago our dishwasher went bad on us and we never replaced it so it became an empty space in our kitchen. The last couple weeks McGwire spent a lot of time hiding in that little cubby hole.

I went to him and said, "We have to do this." I know deep down inside you don't feel well and Mommy wants to help you." He shook his head no and started crying. My Mom came over and bent down to his level and said, "I'll tell ya what McGwire, you can go to my house for a little bit and we'll get ready over there with Papaw." He gave in and said, "Ok." Mom winked at me and whispered, "I'll get him ready over there so be ready at seven o'clock." I said, "Ok." As McGwire left with my mom, I got myself ready but I felt numb.

I was so tired and emotionally drained. I got Larkin out of bed and fed him and we were ready to go. My Dad pulled in with McGwire and my Mom. Patrick, Larkin and I climbed into my dad's truck and we headed to Zanesville to the Urgent Care. It was snowing like crazy and we had a forty-five minute trip to the Doctors office and McGwire wasn't having it. He was angry he had to go. When we finally arrived, we pulled into the parking lot and it was approximately 7:45. I was glad we were early. There was only one other car there. A woman got out of her vehicle to check if they were open. She pulled on the handle of the door, it didn't open so we had to wait until they came out to unlock it. It was freezing outside so the other lady headed back to her car.

Waiting for fifteen minutes felt like forever, I just wanted to get McGwire in there to be seen so we could figure this out. We just needed help so this nightmare would be over. I kept my eyes fixated on the door waiting for it to open. Suddenly I saw one of the office ladies come over and unlock the door. I was ready, I unbuckled my seat belt and jumped out of the truck and ran to the door. My mission was to get McGwire seen as soon as possible and nothing was going to stand in my way. I flew through the door and walked into the office and signed McGwire in. When I turned around to have a seat, the other lady was standing behind me with her son. I made eye contact with her and gave her a polite smile and she gave me a cold look. I didn't understand what that was about, but I didn't have any energy in me to care.

My family came in shortly after I did and sat down. I took Larkin from Patrick and sat down by McGwire. I began to rub McGwire's back and he looked at me mean and got up and moved closer to my Mom trying to avoid me. I hated that he wouldn't let me do things like that anymore. I couldn't sit still, I was too nervous. I paced around the room as I bounced Larkin around on my hip. I was ready to go back to see the doctor now. It was taking forever.

Then suddenly I noticed the other lady got up out of her seat and went up to the window to talk to the receptionist. She said, "Ma'am I just wanted to be clear on something. I was the first to pull into this parking lot before this family over here", as she pointed her finger at me. She said, "That lady over there came running in and signed in first and I don't think that is fair. I know this is a first come first serve basis so I believe my son should be seen first since we arrived first." I couldn't believe what I was hearing. My emotions were so high, I instantly got upset. Inside I was mad but my anger came out in tears. I was trying to compose myself but I was emotionally burnt.

As she sat down, she looked over at me with anger and I quickly turned my head and avoided eye contact. I was frustrated, I didn't need this right now. I'm a people pleaser. I can't stand when someone is upset with me. I didn't even know this lady but I didn't want her to be mad at me. I thought to myself, I didn't rush in here to be rude, if she only knew what we were going through, she would have ran to those doors too. I chose to brush it off and ignore her.

I began to pace faster and faster around the waiting room. Nothing was happening, they were not calling anybody back. I thought, what was the hold up? I noticed the other lady was fidgiting in her chair. She was getting impatient and then suddenly she went back up to the window where the receptionist sat. She knocked on the window and they opened it up and said, "Can I help you?" She said, "Yes, I need to get my son in as soon as possible, we have somewhere we need to be. I just wanted to make sure the doctor is going to see my son first because we were here first." I could tell the receptionist was irritated with her but yet she was being professional and said, "Ma'am, we will get your son back as soon as possible."

The lady went back to her seat and gave me an evil stare down and I turned my head and looked down trying to compose myself. I didn't need this lady today, she was too much for me. I wanted my son back to see the doctor as soon as possible but it didn't have to be like this. Why was she turning this into a childish game? My only focus was on my son who was sitting there desperately needing help. I was angry but my emotions came out in tears. I couldn't hold them back and the lady didn't care. I didn't want her to feel bad for me but she didn't realize what she was doing to my family.

The only thing she cared about was getting to her next event but the only thing I cared about was getting some answers. I began to play the poor me card. I thought to myself, does this lady even know what we've been through these last couple weeks? Has she been up all night worrying about what's wrong with her son? Has she lost sleep by spending all night reciting story after story to get her child to go to sleep because of the torment inside his head? Has she been watching her son suffer day after day? Is she trying everything she can to get through to him? Is she giving her all but constantly falling short? Has she walked a mile in my shoes? Has she lost all control? Is she failing as a Mother? Is she trapped in this nightmare like we are? Is this her story? Maybe it is, I don't know, but I know it's my story and I wish it wasn't.

Maybe she is fighting too or maybe she is lost like me or maybe she just needs to get to a basketball game or something? I don't know her story but all I knew was that she was standing in the way of my son seeing the doctor. Why was I letting this lady get to me? Why was I so upset with her? I needed to refocus myself.

We were at the doctor's office and we were moments away from getting answers so I needed to calm myself down and not let this lady interfere with that. I was just feeling bad for myself and more than that I was feeling bad for my pale faced son sitting there stuck in his head. He wasn't smiling, he didn't look happy and I strive to make my kids happy and I didn't know how to make him happy anymore. I was getting antsy. I glanced over at the lady and I could tell she was still angry with me and I felt bad about it. Maybe I was being selfish but I was fighting for my son and everything around me didn't matter.

I was on a mission and I was going to complete my mission whether it took a battle to get there or not. We all have stories and maybe she had one too but my story was becoming a nightmare and I was looking for a happy ending. I was stuck between this lady and the doctor and I was tired of fighting, I just needed to get through those doors but she was just another roadblock in my way. I didn't want a conflict, that was the last thing I needed. Maybe I did run into this doctor's office as fast as I could to sign McGwire in but it was because I was desperate for help, I saw my opening and I took it. This lady wasn't in my vision because it was just about my son and seeking help.

Sometimes when we find ourselves in these desperate moments, we lose the concept of everything going on around us. We develop tunnel vision. We can only see what is in front of us and everything else around us is a blurr. This lady wasn't on my path, but unfortunately our paths merged together but I do believe it was all for a reason. The nurse finally came back, the other lady looked at me and I looked back at her and then we both looked back at the nurse waiting to see who she was going to call back first. Suddenly the nurse called the name of the other lady's son.

The lady got up, grabbed her purse and gestured for her son to come on and walked towards the nurse and gave me one last cold look with a grin confirming that she got her way. I looked back at her with tears slowly rolling down my face. I didn't say anything, I couldn't, I just spoke it through my tears.

My point to this story is maybe you have been praying and doing all the steps it takes to get that miracle you have been waiting for but God will allow you to watch someone else get that breakthrough. These moments in our lives are hard because when you're going through something like this in your life, seeing someone else get the miracle that you have been praying for will test your faith.

How do you hold on to your faith in God when he allows these things to happen right in front of you? It's hard to trust in God when he blesses someone else but not you. The big question here is why does He allow this to happen? The answer to that question is God is more concerned about your heart than He is about your situation. It was part of God's perfect plan. God placed this lady on my path to grow something deeper inside me that was weak.

God will use difficult people as a tool to structure something bigger in you. This lady was the resistance that God applied to me to strengthen my patience. I have never been a patient person but that day God tested me on a whole new level. I was in training but I didn't even know it at the time. God was also working on my compassion. I have always been a compassionate person but can I be compassionate with someone who is difficult?

It's really easy to be compassionate with someone that is nice, but can I be compassionate with someone that is mean? These are things that God needs to strengthen in us and this is how He does it. The reason we don't understand it at the moment is because we don't realize we are in training. God doesn't tell us we're in training, He just trains us. He will use hard moments like this, that we would never choose for ourselves to strengthen us.

These are the moments when we get angry with God, but these are also the moments God is building us up for our purpose. I relate to this because when I am training someone in my gym, I might ask them to do one more superset of ten bicep curls and ten tricep extensions. They usually look at me like I'm crazy because they already did three sets, but I know it's that fourth set that will make them stronger. Whether I want to admit this or not, this lady in the doctor's office was a special tool God was using. She was the resistance that God applied to strengthen my weak spots. God strengthened my patience and my heart that day.

Now, looking back at this situation, I'm happy He did because when I train someone in my gym, they may not be having a good day. They may be going through something hard and may be angry or maybe they're sad. Maybe they won't be able to bring themselves to train that day but maybe they need to talk instead. God was showing me that I needed to be patient with people and not get in a hurry with everything. I need to slow down and focus on the moment and if that means to sit down by someone and rub their back and talk to them instead of placing them on the treadmill, then I do that. If our training session turns into a therapy session then that's ok.

God allowed this moment in my life to train me to be the personal trainer I am today. God taught me that it's not about what we workout on the outside as much as it is about what we workout on the inside. It's more about the heart. This lady got to go back to see the doctor first. I felt like it wasn't fair. The doctor got to evaluate her son first while mine continued to wait in the waiting room. That lady won the competition that I wasn't trying to have. She won the battle, the battle I wasn't trying to fight. What do you do when someone else gets what you want or what you need? What do you do when someone else gets their prayers answered first and you have to continue waiting? How do you handle that?

My suggestion is keep waiting, keep asking, keep believing, because eventually the nurse will call you back too. Instead of focusing on the fact they got their miracle as you continue to wait for yours, focus on this instead, if God can do it for them then He can do it for you too. God will do it for you but if He blesses someone else first it's because He is building you up for something bigger. A lot of times God's delay is for a bigger display. Finally after waiting for so long, the nurse called McGwire back, it was our turn.

As the nurse walked us back, she asked us a few questions. I answered all her questions and walked her through everything that was going on. I told her about all of McGwire's symptoms and she charted everything and told us the doctor would be in shortly. I felt relieved but scared all at the same time. Finally the doctor came in and joked around with McGwire and said "How are you doing today young man." He would always take a look in McGwire's ears and say, "Do you have potatoes growing in your ears?" McGwire usually laughed but this time he just shrugged his shoulders.

The doctor looked at me and said, "What brought you in today Mom?" I said with tears in my eyes, "It's been a rough couple of weeks honestly." I explained everything to him. He looked at McGwire's chart and said, "It says McGwire was recently treated for strep." I said, "Yes, that is actually what I wanted to ask you about." I said "McGwire has been showing symptoms for a condition called PANDAS. Have you heard of it?" He looked at me and said, "Yes I have but I have never treated anyone with it. I go overseas from time to time and treat strep and it has caused some pretty nasty things to people. It lays dormant in the gut and it can cause a lot of issues. The thing is, it's difficult to diagnose. Let's get his blood drawn and see if strep is still detected in his blood. What I will do is treat him with a long term dose of antibiotic and put him on a steroid and see what that does. We will follow up with him in two weeks."

That evening I did my usual routine of getting McGwire to go to sleep. As I layed down in my bed that night, I reflected on our day, I was living a nightmare. I wanted to pinch myself so I would wake up but I knew it wouldn't do any good because I knew it was all too real. I began to cry hard and I couldn't take the reality of what was happening. I started to pray. I was crying at first but I found myself getting mad as I prayed. I was so frustrated.

My prayer came out aggressively. I said, "Why God, why my son." I was mad at God for letting this happen. I cried harder and asked God in a more aggressive way, "Why would you let this happen to my son. I just want him healed, why won't You heal him, why?"

# CHAPTER 23

# Why, God?

When my son was sick and we were in the midst of all this, I didn't understand why it was happening. It happened so fast with no warning. McGwire was changing rapidly and I couldn't stop it. I was beginning to get angry with God because I felt like I was doing my part by praying but God wasn't doing His part by healing. My son continued to lay there suffering. Everynight he fought a battle inside his head. Each day was so long, but the nights were even longer. There was no breakthrough, we only saw darkness, with no evidence of any light shining through.

My prayers weren't working. Days went by and the medication he was on only made him worse. "Why is he not getting better? Why God?" We were not seeing any progress, things were declining and we had nowhere to turn. I continued to pray, but nothing was happening. Did God even hear me? Did he forget about us? Did we even matter to Him? These were my questions. These were my concerns. I was asking but God wasn't responding. I was trying to remain close to God but I found myself falling deeper and deeper in doubt. I wasn't seeing the finish line to my son's sickness.

Sometimes in life to get better, you have to go through the bad first. It doesn't make sense, I know, but it's so true. A lot of times you feel like you are going backwards. We took McGwire to the doctor looking for a breakthrough, thinking we were making progress but in reality McGwire was getting worse than he already was. The medication made him more irritable and his temper got worse. The nightmares and fears were overtaking his mind. It's hard because I wanted to be able to control the situation but I couldn't. I began to wonder if we would be better off taking him off the medication and starting all over. I didn't know what to do. I knew the old ways weren't working either but at that moment the new ways were worse. We were stuck.

I was praying everyday and everynight but I wasn't seeing any progress at all. I felt like I was drifting away from God and falling deeper into my fears. I began to feel sad and angry all at the same time. I was starting to wonder if anything would ever get better. I was losing the confidence of being a mother. Being a mother was my favorite thing in the world. My identity of being a mother was slowly being stripped away from me because I couldn't help my son and I wasn't focused like I wanted to be for Larkin. I needed God but my prayers were growing weak, I began to not be strong enough to pray, I didn't have the words to say anymore. All I had was the question why? Why God? God understands when we ask these questions. He knows we are human and he knows we are at the bottom of ourselves. On one hand I felt guilty for being mad at God, but on the other hand I was mad and I couldn't help it.

It's so hard to understand why God allows these things in our lives and it's even harder to understand why God doesn't answer prayers right away. God understands why we are upset with Him and He knows we don't understand everything and doesn't expect us to. God allows things to remain a mystery and He will unlock the mystery one day, but this is how we grow in our faith. The best thing to know is we are not trapped in all this even though it feels like we are. He is strengthening us. It's so hard to understand this when you are in the midst of your storm.

The best way for me to explain this to you is in the way I understand it the most. I'm a personal trainer so I think of it as a workout. I train people to get stronger. In order to get stronger, you have to apply resistance. To get stronger it's going to be hard work. It may make you sweat a little bit and it might make you out of breath but at the end of the day after the workout is over, you see the benefits from it. You will feel stronger. God is adding resistance to you, He is applying the weight. Your chest might feel heavy and your shoulders may be carrying all the weight of the world on them but if you keep praying God will take that weight from you and hand you back His peace.

God is building you up for something, He is training you for the next step you're about to take, but first you have to get through this step. We are not trapped, we are moving forward into something bigger than us, but God has to make us stronger first before we move into it. The most important thing to understand is God wants us to come to Him with everything: all of our questions and concerns. He wants us to be real with him.

When we talk to God, it's ok to be specific with Him on your requests. It's not selfish at all. God wants you to pray about everything, He wants you to come to Him with all your problems. That being said, your list of requests are important but don't hold on to them too tight because God may ask you to loosen your grip and let go of some things so you can tighten your grip and hold on firm to your faith. Sometimes I focus too much on when and how I want God to do things and I forget the most important part and that is Who is with me and guiding me through everything.

Jesus is guiding us to something bigger than our list of requests could ever be. We often treat God like a Genie in a bottle and we think if we make a wish, God should grant it right away but that's not how it works. We need to know God is listening and He does hear us. I know sometimes we feel like God is answering some other peoples prayers immediately but ours are going unheard. I thought we had McGwire's diagnosis figured out and going to the doctor's office was the answer but yet McGwire was getting worse. I felt like Jesus stopped in His tracks. I thought we were on our way to our breakthrough and this nightmare would be over but it wasn't. I thought I was following Jesus but in reality I was taking the lead.

We should never get ahead of Jesus and lead Him, He needs to lead us. When Jesus stops, we need to stop too. When Jesus moves forward then we have to follow. We have to remain close to Him. We may be asking God hard questions and we may be angry with Him but I have good news, we are where God wants us. God just wants us to talk to Him and rely on Him. You are one step closer than you were before. I wasn't talking to God before my son was sick. I may have prayed to Him occasionally when times got hard but with my son's sickness I began to pray to Him every night.

My prayers with Him sometimes were short because I couldn't find the words to say anymore. The thing is, God knows. It's not always about how much you say as it is more about turning everything over to Him and spending time with Him. God knows what you are trying to say, He hears you even when you can't speak the words. The thing was it felt like God wasn't responding to my prayer requests but in reality He was actually behind the scenes working, I just didn't know it. I was getting to a breaking point but I hadn't dropped to my knees yet. God needs us on our knees, God allows us to hit rock bottom until all we have left is Him. I was almost there but I was still holding onto some things that weren't mine to hold on too. I wasn't ready to fully give McGwire over to Him.

Let's revisit that question: Why God? Why does God allow these things to happen? Why doesn't he answer them right away? Why doesn't God just give us a timeline? God doesn't tell us how long our battles will last. He doesn't give us any indication the end is in sight, why? I know I would be able to handle this battle better if He told me how long it would last or if we were even going to survive this. God doesn't give us a timeline because He's doing something so much bigger. If God gave us everything we asked for right on the spot, we would take it for granted and we would never spend time with Him on those good days. We would only run to Him when we were in trouble and we would never carry on the relationship with Him.

We have to remain close to God and in order to do that we have to lean on Jesus and stop focusing on our fears and put our focus on Him. Fear makes us run away and we have to make a choice, do we drift away or do we lean in and remain close. If God gave us our story before we lived it then we would have no reason to live. We don't want to know how the story ends because we would never have the journey getting there. We would never have the strength to be what we are truly made to be if we didn't have storms God allows in our lives.

If we wrote our own story it would end in tragedy. God is the author of our lives and it will be a perfect ending only if we trust and remain close to jesus. Your story will be told and your testimony will be made. Keep talking to God and keep asking, your prayers will be answered, it just might not be today or tomorrow, it will be on God's perfect timing.

CHAPTER 24

# Why Didn't I Cancel
# My Class?

D uring the time my son was sick, I kept it hidden. I covered up my insecurities. Some people knew my son was sick but not to the extent it truly was. People didn't know what it did to me and my family. People didn't know the impact it had on me and how broken inside I truly was. When I walked into my workout classes I faked a smile, I hid my wounds. I pretended I was fine when I wasn't. I thought I needed to look strong or no one would want to be led by me. I always felt since I instructed workout classes and I'm a trainer that I have to look my part and be strong physically but I also had to be strong emotionally.

My goal was to help others but in reality I was the one who needed help. I needed to talk to someone on the outside of my storm but instead I held it all in. Trust me, not talking to people about what you are going through isn't the answer. The longer you hold it in, the heavier it gets. In reality I was broken, life was hard for me when my son was sick. Countless times I was crying right before I stepped into my class to face everyone. These days I'm an open book. I realized I had it all backwards. If I'm going to help someone, I need to reveal the broken side of me. I realized that when someone is struggling, the last person they want to hear from is someone who has it all together. They want to talk to someone who has been through the storm that they are going through. If they know you can relate to them or they can relate to you, you have a way of getting through to them. They will open up. There is healing when you talk about it and there is also healing when you share your testimony.

I decided to quit focusing on trying to build myself up in other people's eyes and let my guard down and reveal to them my family's story. We need to take our testimony and use it for greater purpose.

The world has taught us to cover up the weak side of ourselves. It's scary to share your testimony at first but the impact you might have on someone's life could be so powerful, it could be life changing. If you show someone what God helped you overcome, it gives people hope that they can overcome their battle too.

Maybe they are barely holding on and about to give up, but maybe it's your testimony that can give them something to hold onto. We strive for perfection, but it's not about perfection. In reality no one is perfect. We all have a purpose in life. We all have experience and we are all gifted somewhere, but at the end of the day it doesn't matter who you are or what you do, we all need someone.

If you are a highly skilled doctor, at some point in your life you will need a doctor to take care of you. If you are an uplifting preacher, at some point you may need to be preached to. In my case, I'm a personal trainer but I need someone to train me, to push me to that next level. I won't push myself like someone else would. My point is, we are placed on this earth to help each other, but you need to share your wounds with someone so they can help you too. Don't do what I did and cover it up, instead open up. Show those scars because likely those scars were placed there to heal others. We have to show people that they are not alone, we all struggle.

When I instruct classes, sometimes I walk around my class as they are working out. If I see someone struggling to get that last rep, I will tell them that they can do it, to not give up, to keep going. That last rep is the one that counts. That last rep is the hardest one and it's the rep you don't feel like doing but it's also the rep that makes you stronger. If you are struggling you are getting stronger. You can't get a testimony until you get a test. It's the resistance applied that strengthens us. If you want to be strong, you have to do the work, you have to do the last rep, even when you don't feel like it.

Working out is just like praying, sometimes we don't feel like praying. Sometimes we feel too weak and too tired to pray to God. Our battles make us weary and short of breath. Our battles are the resistance applied. When we work out, to get stronger, we need to lift. We have to lift those barbells until we can't. We have to lift those dumbbells until we are down to the last rep. We have to lift when we don't feel like it to gain that strength. We have to do the work. The same with praying: to get stronger we need to lift. We have to lift those arms up. We have to stretch our arms up high until we find our strength in God. Lift when you don't want to, that's where the strength comes from.

I like to help people find their strength in my classes but sometimes I work out with them too. This shows people that I feel their struggle. If I workout with them I am relating to what they are going through, because I am going through it with them. They will push harder and find more strength in themselves if they know that someone else is in the battle too. We are under the resistance together. We are working out together, we are lifting together. We are not alone. I won't let anyone feel alone in the struggle of working out in my class, just like God won't let anyone feel alone in the struggle of praying. God is in this with us, He is going through this with us. He meets us where we are. God may have been applying the resistance but He is also helping us learn how to lift something that is heavy, something bigger than us.

My point is we need each other and we need to work through to the last rep, we need the resistance even when it doesn't feel good. Our strength comes from the weight applied and from the work we do even when we don't feel like it. Our strength comes from God. Like I said, I didn't reveal anything to my class when Mcgwrie was sick, I hid it, but my class was my escape from my reality, from my storm. I needed my class more than they ever knew. They were my outlet but I never revealed that to them. Let me give you an illustration.

One evening before one of my workout classes, I was having a hard time getting McGwire to do his homework. I tried to get him to sit down and focus and get it done, but he refused. He never wanted to leave it blank but yet he didn't want to do the work. He never left us with a choice. This would always end in a complete meltdown. This particular night was worse than others.

My mom showed up that evening in the midst of it all. She walked in with McGwire face down on the floor kicking and screaming. Mom bent down to his level and said, "McGwire, look at you, what are you doing?" McGwire screamed saying, "Mommy and Daddy were being mean." She said, "Why, because they are making you do your homework, that's not mean they are doing that because they love you and they want the best for you." Homework never used to be a problem with McGwire but when he was sick, doing any kind of task would cause these meltdowns.

My mom was calm in our storm. She was the only one that McGwire would calm down for. I had a class that evening and it was about to start. McGwire started crying wanting to go to my Moms house. I was frustrated and I said, "Not tonight, it's a school night." He began to drop to his knees again going into another meltdown. I couldn't take another meltdown. I was at the point where I didn't know what to do anymore. McGwire wasn't improving with the medication and he was getting worse as each day went by.

I had enough of it. I said, "McGwire, you are staying home." He said, "This house is a nightmare and I want out of it." Hearing him say that cut into me like a knife. He always loved his home and now it felt like it was a nightmare. My confidence of being a good mother was shattered. I was done. I began to cry. McGwire noticed I was crying and he began to laugh hysterically. There would be times he would do this, just laugh when he shouldn't be laughing. He had his emotions messed up. There would be times he would cry when something funny would happen. I didn't know this at the time but kids with PANDAS often get their emotions confused and will laugh or cry at the wrong times. Everything felt backwards with him. I was so confused about everything. McGwire laughing at me set me over the edge.

I said, "Enough, this has gone on too long. I am taking McGwire to Children's Hospital right now." McGwire started screaming at the top of his lungs, "No!" My mom said, "Cassie, Childrens isn't the answer. They're going to treat him with harsh medications and we don't want to go down that road." I said, "Well then where do we go from here?" She said, "That's why I came over, I wanted to talk to you about a doctor in Columbus that I found. I was researching PANDAS and found a doctor that actually specialized in PANDAS and he treats them with supplements. We need to go see him." I said, "Well let's go there then. "

She said, "We have to schedule an appointment first. We'll talk about this later. I'll show you the video I found on him." She said, "Let me take him to my house for a little bit so I can calm him down and I'll make sure he comes back tonight." I threw my hands up and said, "Fine!" McGwire was smiling happy to leave which broke my heart to see the smile that I couldn't produce anymore. I hated that leaving me brought him happiness. I held back my tears, and fought myself from crying.

My workout class was coming soon so I needed to stay strong. I held it together as McGwire walked out the door. I was tired of him leaving all the time. I felt like an absent Mom. I wanted to be his mom, but he longer let me. He wanted my Mom and not me which hurt so bad. I didn't feel like doing my workout class that night. I was too emotional. I just wanted to hold my son, but that wasn't an option. Even though I didn't feel like doing my class I knew I needed them. They were my distraction from all this. I wanted to cry but I couldn't. In order not to cry I had to produce anger. I didn't want to resort to anger but I had to so I wouldn't cry.

I paced around the house cleaning up everything. Patrick followed me through the house and said, "Cass, do you want to talk about this?" I said, "No, not really." He said, "It's ok to talk about it, it will make you feel better." I said, "I don't want to talk about it." Patrick stopped me in my tracks and grabbed my hand and said, "Cass stop for a second." I forcefully pulled my hand from his and said, "No, I don't have time and this house is a mess, I have to clean it up." I started organizing things that didn't even need to be organized.

I went to the kitchen and started to do the dishes and he followed me and started to dry them. As I handed each dish to him, he looked at me with a concerned face and said "Cass, talk to me." He knew not to ask those three terrible words, "are you ok," because he knew I wasn't ok. He knew if he asked those three words, I would lose it and he knew I was trying to hold it together so I could compose myself for my class.

My phone rang and I saw it was my mom. I answered and in a very monotone voice, my mom said, "Cassie, I just wanted to let you know I got McGwire settled down and it's gonna be ok, just hang in there."

She asked if I had a class that night and I said I did. She said "Cass, why don't you just cancel it for tonight so you can rest. I'm worried about you. You just need time to absorb all this. Just take tonight off. You're going through a lot and you're just going to wear yourself out." I said, "I know Mom and I appreciate it but I need to do this class. I need a distraction from all this." She said, "Just please consider it. You don't have to run on fumes like this, try to rest. You need to relax and take some time off." I said, "Mom, I can't. I know you don't understand but these people help me. I need them more than I need rest."

My mom says I am die hard, I get it from my dad. If he wants to do something or if he feels it's important, he will do it no matter what. Even if he is tired or had a long day or in my case even if he is slowly breaking apart piece by piece. My dad and I are both like this. Why? For me, the reason is because people matter to me. I don't like to let people down.

When someone comes into my life, I will make sure I am there for them no matter what. That night I didn't cancel my class because what if they needed to talk? What if they were having a bad day like I was? What if they waited all day to come to my class so they could blow off some steam? What if I was their lifeline that night? What if they were my lifeline? What if they were the only thing I felt I had? Yeah I know it's a bunch of "what ifs", but the what ifs are enough for me to not let go. They are enough for me to step into that class even if I'm not okay. I wasn't okay but I had them and I needed them that night.

My class isn't just a class to me, it's my outlet and those people are my friends, they're like family. I was falling deep into "the pit" that night and I needed a rope to climb back out. My class was that rope for me and I was counting on that, maybe I was the rope for them. I needed people to talk to and be with, not a pillow to cry into. Drowning in my sorrows wasn't the answer: being with people and helping someone else was.

When my son was sick, there were times I didn't want to do anything but lay around lost in my sorrows. I wanted to give up. I was so tired and drained it was really hard to compose myself enough to find the energy to get up and instruct a class but I knew deep down it's what I needed. I had to get up because I needed something else to walk into that was calm rather than staying in the war inside my house. I needed hope but dealing with the pain of seeing my son fall apart was defeating me. As bad as I wanted to cancel my class and give up, there was something inside me that pushed me to rise above.

I needed to help someone even though it was me that truly needed the help. I really believe the reason why I felt the need to help someone else was because I couldn't help my son. I had to make a choice that night: do I cancel my class or do I instruct it? If I cancel, will the fear take over and corrupt my mind? Will I sink further down in the pit? If I instruct my class, will I be able to be strong enough for them? Will I have it in me to give my class what they need? I didn't know the answers but I chose to instruct the class that night because I needed them and they needed me.

The next question is: how do you turn off one emotion and turn on a new one? How do you pull it all together enough to face people when the only emotion you have is sadness? How do you fake a smile when you struggle producing one? How do you help people overcome their battles when you are still in the midst of yours? These are hard questions and I really don't have an answer for them. The only answer I have is "Sometimes when you don't feel like doing something but you know you should, do it anyway. If you feel like you don't have enough willpower to do it, or strength inside you, use what you have and God will give you the rest of His strength."

I decided that I will help people overcome their battles even though I was still in mine. I wanted to listen to people and help encourage them through their battles but what they didn't know was that I was walking back inside to face my own battle. It's weird how you can help people when you need help. It's probably because you relate to them. You understand what they are going through. There is true healing when you help people through a storm because in some ways it helps you.

The big thing I want you to understand is don't let the enemy win. Just because you are struggling doesn't mean you can't help another person. There are going to be times we don't feel like doing something but it doesn't mean you can't. Try not to operate off of feelings, because feelings will only get you so far and if you guide yourself through feelings, you will eventually hit a dead end road. Try to operate off of hope and use the faith you have even if it doesn't feel like you have enough. I learned that when you need help, and you feel lost, there is healing in helping others. Sometimes the advice we pour out to someone is the advice you need for yourself. Or maybe someone else's situation can help you in yours. Or maybe the people you surround yourself with can help you get out of the pit you're stuck in.

Rise up and go. I know you don't feel like going because you feel numb, and you don't want to be around people but I promise if you help somebody in the midst of your storm, your storm will calm a little. The wind will slow down just enough for you to stand steady and the fog will separate. The path will look more clear, so go find that person and help them, and maybe they will help you too.

As I walked into my class that night, I put on a happy face to cover up the sorrow inside me. I might have been hiding behind a mask, but I had to be able to compose myself. My class was put there for my healing. I remember laughing that night, honest laughing. My class was able to put a smile on my face, a real actual smile. A smile I couldn't produce myself. They didn't know behind my smile there was so much pain.

When we started the class, I was sad. The only thing I could think about was McGwire's sick, pale face. I had to escape my thoughts by pushing harder. My stress made us move faster and faster, because I needed to sweat my emotions out and leave them to rest on the basement floor.

At that moment, I was able to forget for a second. I got lost in the workout, lost in the music. My drive came from my battle. My strength came from moving forward and not giving up. The workout was for them, but it was also for me to numb my pain for forty-five minutes as we pushed. The sadness was still there, but I was dragging it to its grave, I was burying it, it no longer had control over me. I was walking forward into something I didn't feel like doing but I did it anyway. We have to push through the pain and go when we need to go and stop when we need to stop. Maybe I should have canceled my class that night but I knew that I was supposed to move forward into it. You are too.

You need to move forward into something you don't feel like doing. You will know whether you should go because you will feel the urge deep inside of you pushing you forward. You will also feel something trying to hold you back but don't let it win. That workout took me to the next step on my path and it will take you to the next step too.

My feelings were raw.

That evening after class, I had to fight to get McGwire home from my Moms. After getting him to bed. I went to my bed and laid down and reflected on my day. I couldn't sleep. My feelings were raw. I thought to myself, "Why was this defeating me? Why do I feel so weak? I thought I was stronger than this. Why does it feel like I can't breathe anymore? I'm alive but why do I feel lifeless and in a daze? Why was this put upon me and my family? Why were we still dealing with this? Why won't God heal my son and make this all go away?"

Being a mom was my favorite thing in life but I didn't feel like a good mom anymore. I was so vulnerable. As a family we were falling apart and I've never been good at puzzles so I knew I couldn't put the pieces back together. I knew I needed God to do it for me. I was holding on to my son so tight but I was slowly losing grip of him. He was slipping away from me and that scared me so much. I was trying to keep my faith that God would help us but I was questioning things.

My faith was diminishing and I was losing all hope. I was trying to keep a positive outlook on everything but I was constantly falling short, not able to complete my mission of being the mom that fixes everything. I couldn't fix this one and I knew it, and I hated to admit that. I was so used to being able to do it all on my own, but I couldn't do this. I was defeated. I knew deep down all I had left was to surrender. The burdens laid on my chest so deep, I couldn't explain it.

Words can't express the pain I felt. I knew this was something I needed to let go of and hand it over to God, but I found myself holding on to it and not ready to let go. This storm was bigger than me. I was stuck. I felt pulled between two barriers, letting go or holding on. Losing the chains I was bound to or tightening them. Surrendering made me feel like I lost the battle but in reality surrendering is when you finally win. I didn't want to give up on my son. I wasn't a quitter but I knew I needed to hand this over to God, but how?

# CHAPTER 25

# Bent Knees

How do you hand your children over to God? It's not that easy. It's easy to hand over things to Him that don't really matter to you, but your child? No way. I couldn't let go of my children. When I first held my boys in my arms I promised them I would never let go. I would always be there for them no matter what. If I had to pick the words to define who I am in this world it would be that I am a mother of two amazing boys. That's how I define myself, a mother. At least that's how I used to define myself but I know that if we peel back layer after layer of things we define ourselves as, what do we have left?

We can define ourselves as a lot of things in this world, but what are we truely? We are the children of God. God is our Father and we need to define ourselves as children of God before anything else. Handing your children over to God doesn't mean you are giving up on them and it doesn't mean that you're not their mother or father anymore. It just simply means you are letting Him take the wheel so you don't have to have all the weight of the world on your shoulders. At this moment in time, I felt that handing my boys over to God was out of the question. I couldn't do it. I would give Him anything, but not my boys. They were mine. How do you let go of something that you have been holding onto so tight and let God take it over? The answer to that is further down this backroad. I wasn't ready to hand them over yet and maybe you're not either so let's keep exploring down this road and see how we're going to get there together.

At this point in the journey my world was shaken and I couldn't stand steady on two feet without stumbling. The earthquake set in without any warning whatsoever. I wasn't ready and because of it I fell hard crashing to the ground and found myself face down in the dirt. I couldn't focus on tasks or conservations because all I did was worry. My mind was crowded, I couldn't think or process anything but the storm. I woke up worrying and went to bed worrying. If you're really good at worrying, like I was, you would be amazing at praying. I wish someone would have told me that, but even if they did, I probably wouldn't have listened because anxiety had control over me.

I spent a lot of time fearing the worst and took myself to a dark place that I shouldn't have ever been. I was always thinking of the worst case scenarios. Maybe I did that to prepare myself for the worst, but I believe that kind of thinking only pushed me further into fear than I would have been if I had just put it in God's hands. Worrying causes a lot of emotions that can get out of control. There's a sense of peace that prayer gives.

God gave us an imagination starting as young children, but we lose grip of it as we grow older. God gave us an imagination to serve the purpose of faith, but we end up using our imaginations to take us down the dead roads of fear. We have to get our imaginations back to childlike faith so we walk down the right path. You have to let go of some things, and put everything in God's hands. It's not easy to let go of stuff you have been holding onto for so long. We get into protective mode and we hold on tight to these things because we believe we need them to get by. God will sometimes have us let go of people or things in our lives to get us ready for the space He is taking us into. We have to decrease and let go so God can increase and take over.

You might feel like you are living in an earthquake but God has to shake things up so He can shake those things out that you were depending on that kept you from depending on Him. We need people and things in life that we can actually depend on, not people or things we have been hiding behind. If God doesn't shake things out that you have been depending on then you will sabotage what He is trying to do inside you. He is helping you grow. Why do we fight it? We need to trust God and trust His process. I didn't know that at the time. I felt hopeless, weak and vulnerable. I was riding the waves of doubt.

The tension I was under was driving out my faith, or so I thought, in reality it was driving it in. The tension was strengthening me but

I didn't see it that way. I was quitting without even trying anymore. Let me tell you something, when you have been under something that is so painful for so long, it will knock the wind out of you. You will feel like you can't remember what it feels like to breathe anymore. You will feel defeated and broken. You will want to give up, but don't because this is where the enemy wants you. Don't give up, but instead give in, give in to God and hand those things over to Him and He will give you His peace.

If you don't hand things over, negativity will set in and take over. When you spend so long in the negative state, it will consume you and that's what you will become. Your mind will only be able to process everything in a negative way. You will adapt to all the insecurities you have. This will cause you to become cold, hard and bitter because you won't see things any other way. You won't be able to see the good things in life because you will end up adapting to the bad. When you feel trapped and blinded by your storm, the whirlwind will fog your vision from seeing the good in anything. This happened to me and maybe it's happening to you, but God is calling you to rise up out of this. He is calling you to step up and be the person that He sees, not the person that you think you are.

You are bigger than your storm but the enemy is working overtime trying to convince you otherwise. We need to start to see who we are through the lens of what God sees and not through the lens of the storm we are in. We define ourselves according to our battle, but we have to see ourselves as the potential of rising up from it. The storm isn't dragging us down like we think it is. In reality, our storm is building us up for something great. But you have to see it the way God sees it.

Don't operate from feelings or emotions, they will take you down a dead end road. You have to operate from the devotion of God guiding you. God wouldn't be allowing this in your life if He wasn't intending to use it. Satan wouldn't be placing the storm on you if he didn't see you as a threat. Don't be scared anymore because Satan is the one who is truly scared. He is just trying to convince you that you're the one who should be scared. Satan sends a storm to knock us off our feet. God uses the storm to strengthen us to be the warrior He sees us as.

Pain can really weigh a person down. Waking up everyday with a burden or pain that won't go away can really stand in the way of moving forward. We have to stay positive through these times of uncertainty. We reach our breaking points when pain gets to be too much and we can't handle it anymore. Sometimes we take two steps forward and then a giant leap back. It's ok when we fall back, because if we fall backwards the only way to look is up. If you are looking up then you are seeking God.

We want to be healed from our problems but sometimes it takes a lot longer than we expect. We want a diagnosis, we need answers. McGwire had a diagnosis but we didn't have answers yet. I was scared of the diagnosis because I didn't know what road we were headed down and I had no reference to how long it was going to take. Maybe it's not the diagnosis that we should fear. What if the diagnosis wasn't about the fears, but what if it was more about the journey of getting there? What if the diagnosis was the process of finding a new strength we never knew we had inside of us? What if the diagnosis was the path we took that led us to our new and improved destination? What if God was leading us somewhere bigger than we could ever imagine?

It's hard not to focus on the diagnosis and where it might lead us. We can't get a diagnosis and instantly put ourselves in a grave because I'm here to tell you, that grave couldn't hold the power of Jesus and it can't hold you either when you have the power of Jesus inside you. Sometimes it's the journey that heals you, the walk through the fire that you will find your answers. That being said, the journey isn't going to be a walk in the park.

You will stumble on the way. You may fall, but you have to get back up and try again because one foot after the other will get you through the process and you will find your healing on the way there. When you're walking through this journey you'll feel weak, so you'll need God's power. When I train someone, I try to find where they are weak and when I discover their weaknesses I will spend a lot of time trying to help them strengthen those weak spots. God does the same thing with us.

He will find where we are weak and He will start to do work within us. When I'm training people and have them do a workout that they struggle with, they usually don't like it because it's too difficult for them. I don't pick the workouts that they struggle with to be mean to them, I pick them because as a trainer I know what's best for them. I know the root of most of their problems comes from those weak spots. God knows what's best for us too. When we get hit with a storm that is difficult, we often blame God for it, but the storms are God's way of giving us a workout. He is training us for the next step in our lives. A lot of times I have high school students come to me wanting me to train them for a specific sport. I will evaluate them and look for the areas that they need to work on to improve the mechanics for that certain sport.

If they want to be successful in that sport they have to train for it in a specific way and strengthen specific muscles for it. I will train a baseball player differently than I would train a football player because of the mechanics of the sport. I may also train two football players that are training for the same position a little differently because one may be weak in their hamstrings while the other might be weak in their quadriceps. We can't compare our problems in life to other people's problems because we are all being trained by God in a specific way.

These students that I train would never be ready without proper training. They have to train to be successful. I tell them all the time that it has to hurt in order to make it to the next step. The pain we feel is the gains we make. If you feel like you can't do it now, don't give up because soon you will be strong enough to do it. I tell them don't give up on me because I won't give up on you. You may not believe in yourself but I believe you. I wouldn't be pushing you the way I do if I didn't think you could do it. I see something in you that you can't see. You think you can't but I know you can. This is how God feels about us.

He knows our future and the potential we have but we are blinded by our storm just like my athletes are blinded by the workout. If the workout is geared around their weaknesses they want to give up, but they don't realize they are transforming their weaknesses to strengths. Our storms usually are geared around our weaknesses too and that's why we want to give up so soon. I push the athletes so when the competition comes they will be ready. I will train the students several months before their season starts so they don't come into it weak. They have to walk into the competition stronger than they were before. They have to gain their confidence and be ready to fight. God is training you in a specific way to get you ready for where He is taking you.

He is taking you somewhere that feels bigger than you, but in reality He is taking you to your purpose, God is leading you to your dreams. You have to trust Him and trust the process, but I promise you the storm is the workout and that is why we struggle. I know the storm you are going through is difficult and you want it to be over. When I am training someone, they want the workout to be over. When the workout is finally over they feel stronger coming out of it.

Everytime when they come in and do the workout, they walk out with a new kind of power that they didn't have before. This is what God is doing to you right now. If you are struggling you are gaining something bigger than your problems. This struggle means God is choosing you. He picked you and now it's time to rise out of it with power.

The next question is how? How do you rise out of your storm with power? Where does the power come from? The power comes from your knees. It comes from being weak and having nothing left except dropping to your knees and surrendering to God. Why? Because that's where God needs us. He needs us to fall so He can pick us up. The only way to rise out of something is to fall. If you want to see God's power, you have to get down on your knees and pray.

There is power that comes from your bent knees. A lot of people I train are weak in their shoulders. There are a lot of workouts that you can do to strengthen the shoulders but in my opinion shoulder presses are one of the hardest lifts you can do. If your shoulders are weak, doing shoulder presses can be tough. When I see people struggle with shoulder presses, I tell them they can do push presses instead.

Push presses are a press that allows you to bend your knees to help generate more power to lift the barbell over your head. Push presses allow the legs to help so there isn't so much weight on the shoulders. My point is during the storms we carry the weight of the world on our shoulders but we don't have to. We have someone to help generate more power so we can lift our arms up and reach for help. We have the choice to bend our knees. If you feel like you have tried everything and you have nothing left, my suggestion is to go ahead and fall on your knees.

Use your knees, lift your arms up, and reach for the One who can help. Reach for the One who carries the power. Reach for God and He can lift the weight off of your shoulders and give you His peace. The bigger the pain, the bigger the gain. The heavier the weight, the bigger the blessing. The blessing is hidden behind the process, keep working and those weak areas will soon turn into your strengths. If life gets too hard and you feel weak drop down on your knees when you feel like you can't stand anymore. Don't be afraid to get those knees dirty because you will find the power to get back up.

# CHAPTER 26

# The 7 Year Gap

D ay in and day out McGwire began to change. The steroid continued to make him worse. We had our follow up appointment with McGwire's doctor and he decided to take him off of the steroid, but he left him on the antibiotic. The doctor wasn't sure what to do. PANDAS was too new and he didn't know enough about it or how to treat it. He was guiding us towards Children's Hospital. He felt they could do counseling with him and treat him as if he had OCD. This was not the answer I wanted.

I felt like no one could help us. We went home with no answers. I did a lot of research on PANDAS but there wasn't much information on how to help McGwire get better. I didn't want to go down the road of counseling and harsh mediations, especially at his age. McGwire was pulling away from me and began to drift closer into my moms loving arms. On one hand, it was reassuring to me that he had her, but on the other hand, I just needed to wrap my arms around him and tell him I loved him and that he was going to be ok, but he wouldn't let me do that. I just had to watch him decline and it hurt so bad. It was so painful to not be able to do anything. As much as I tried, I couldn't control this, it was out of my hands.

Everyday began to feel like a struggle just to get out of bed. I felt as if I was trapped in a nightmare that I couldn't escape. My son was so different. He changed so much and I just wanted to wake up one day and everything be back to normal. Instead I woke up every day to a new child, a child I didn't know anymore. I felt myself shutting down wanting to give up because the dark was consuming me. The mornings were long and the evenings were even longer. Each day became harder. I was slowly breaking apart.

Getting up every morning consisted of McGwire crying wanting to go to my mom's house. I began to not fight it anymore because it just caused too much havoc in the house and Larkin didn't need to see that. I was getting weak and the fight wasn't worth it. I had to pick my battles and this was a battle I couldn't win. As hard as I tried, my son just didn't want me to help him, but I desperately wanted to help him. Our family was breaking apart piece by piece. My mom lived next door and she would come pick up McGwire and he would stay there all day. It was really hard to let him go, but I had to. I was so used to him being home by my side all day. I was so used to creating adventures for us. We used to have so much fun.

I felt like those days were over. In the blink of an eye, they were gone. I began to think how long is this going to go on? When will it be over? Once McGwire went to my moms, it was really hard to get him to come back home. It began to kill me inside. I wanted my boy back. He stayed at my mom's house a lot. I felt like an absent Mom and it wasn't my choice. I was used to tucking him in and kissing him goodnight and I didn't have that anymore. Those days bedtime consisted of screaming and crying all night long. I started to panic the closer it got to bedtime because it was such a scary time for all of us.

I had to prepare and create bedtime stories from the top of my head. When McGwire would stay at moms house, I got a break from all that, but it was bittersweet. I hated all the screaming and having to create story after story, but when he wasn't home I missed that. I was incomplete without him home. I felt like I wasn't doing my job of being the Mom he needed and I was giving up on him. The stories were all I had, they were the only thing McGwire let me do.

His absence left me feeling empty, I had no purpose. Larkin was the only thing I had to hold onto. When McGwire was gone, I found myself holding Larkin all the time, I never wanted to let go of him. I thought at least I had him to hold, but I needed both of my boys to feel complete. It felt so comforting to rock Larkin in our chair, but I found myself not able to focus on anything because I was lost in my thoughts. I was so distracted I couldn't turn off my mind from the reality of what was going on with McGwire. I needed to get to the bottom of all this and get my boy back.

I often wondered why there was a seven year gap between my two boys. If it was up to me there would have been a two year gap. The thing is it wasn't up to us, it was God's perfect timing. When McGwire turned one, my husband and I discussed it and agreed it was time to have another child. We had a plan. As time went by, and McGwire turned three, the gap between our next child was getting bigger than we wanted, but we never gave up hope. Time kept slipping away and we continued to try, but I just couldn't get pregnant. We tried everything but it just wasn't happening. Life got busy and time slipped away.

McGwire started school and we accepted that he was going to be our only child. McGwire always talked about wanting a little baby brother or sister. I felt bad that he was lonely. To fill that void, I took it upon myself to use every free moment I had to play with him. I felt guilty that he didn't have a sibling to play with. McGwire and I became very close. Our bond grew more and more everyday. I was his mother, but we were also best friends. McGwire and I did everything together. When I got home from work, my focus was him. I put everything on hold that I needed to do so I could play with my boy. He was my everything, he was my life, my only child. I was determined I was going to be the best mom I could be.

When McGwire started to learn how to write words, he became fascinated with writing books. We would fold a few pieces of paper together and staple them. We would sit down and create our own mini books. McGwire would Illustrate the pictures and I would write the story to go along with the picture he had drawn. We would get lost in our own little world and do this for hours. We had so much fun! We have a big bag full of all these stories. Recently while going through things and organizing the house, I came across those mini books and sat down and read them to McGwire and Larkin. It was so special to spend the evening reminiscing with McGwire about those special memories and little Larkin loved listening to our stories.

I believe while creating those stories with McGwire, God was preparing us for the stories I had to create for the long nights of fighting demons in McGwire's head. I didn't have much I could do to help McGwire during his sickness, but I had the stories. Who knew when we were writing these mini books, we were preparing for the storm we were facing. I guess this is why things hurt so bad for me because the bond McGwire and I had built through the years was broken. It was shattered and I didn't know how to put it back together. This is why it was so hard for me to be pushed away from my son when he became sick.

As McGwire grew, my husband and I gave up on all hopes of having another child. Until one day I wasn't feeling well and I decided to take a pregnancy test and it was positive. McGwire and Patrcik were sitting in the living room and I came running out of the bathroom crying. McGwire and Patrick looked at me and I said I'm pregnant! McGwire jumped up and down with excitement and Patrick gave me a big hug. I could see it in Patricks eyes, he was emotional too. We were not prepared for this. We had already gotten rid of all of McGwire's baby stuff, so we had to start all over again. We didn't care! We were so happy to finally have another child. The day little Larkin was born and placed in my arms and my eyes locked with his, I knew he was my miracle baby. I loved him so much and when McGwire held him for the first time the bond was built, he finally had a little brother.

McGwire was seven and he was ready to be the big brother. Let's go back to the question: Why was there a seven year gap? Why did it take so long to have Larkin? God has His reasons, but I believe God revealed the answer to me for the purpose of this book. It's an important aspect to understand, so let me walk you through it. First of all, God knows what we don't know and one thing God knew that I didn't was my son McGwire was going to get sick. God knew the bond McGwire and I had and God also knew McGwire was going to shut down and push me away. He also knew there would be alot of tears, heartache and pain that was going to go along with all of this.

God knew I was going to need a cushion, and little Larkin was going to be the cushion I needed. When things got hard and McGwire wasn't there, I had Larkin to hold and comfort me. The days I wanted to give up, Larkin was always there for me. On the days I felt I was failing at being a mom, I had Larkin to hold and remind me I had something worth fighting for. When I felt sad and McGwire was with my Mom, Larkin was there for me to rock. As I rocked him and looked deep into his dark chocolate eyes, he would smile and that made me smile. It was like he knew I needed him. I would draw Larkin close to me to fill the void of McGwire not letting me hold him.

I had my baby boy Larkin to comfort me. Larkin was one, he was my cuddly baby, my security blanket. If God allowed him to be born on my terms he would have been six during all of this. The problem with that is, he would have memories of everything. He would have the trauma that went along with all of this. He would remember all the screaming, tantrums, crying, and the nightmares. We shielded Larkin as much as we could through this, by taking him in another room with either myself or Patrick while the other one dealt with McGwire.

With Larkin being one, he has no memory or trauma and I'm so thankful for that. For all these years I questioned God why? Why a seven year gap? As I write this story today, I answered my own question. This is an illustration of why God does things on His own timing and not ours because God knows all. Seven is the number of heaven, it's the number of completion and He placed Larkin in our lives just at the right time, but I never saw it that way until now. Larkin gave me a reason to not give up and here's a story to show you how.

I can remember one day in particular that McGwire didn't want to come home. I called my Mom asking for him to come home. He had been there a lot and I was tired of it. I felt like I was giving up on being his mother and I couldn't do it anymore. I needed him home. I started crying uncontrollably and asked my Mom, "why doesn't he want to come home? He used to love being home. Why doesn't he want to be with me anymore? Why won't he let me hold him? Why is this all happening Mom? Why? This isn't fair. I'm a mom that wants to be a mom. I just want to hug him and tell him I love him but he won't let me. Is this how it's going to be forever? Will I ever get him back? What did I ever do to deserve this? I have always been there for him. I have been a fully committed mom to him, I was his best friend.

Why has this all changed? I was always his comforter when he was hurt. I was the one who rubbed his back to say it's going to be ok. He won't let me do that anymore. I need him home Mom, I have to have him here, even if he doesn't want to be here. I can't do this anymore." I know this hurt my mom, I could hear the strain in her voice as she spoke. She was stuck. On one hand she had my son because he wanted her and not me. She had to be the comforter because she was the only one he allowed to do it. On the other hand, she had me, her daughter, who was in so much pain crying desperately to get her son back. She didn't want to keep him from me. She didn't want to see me like this, but she didn't want to see McGwire hurting like he was either. She didn't know what to do. She was torn. I didn't want to hurt her, I didn't want her to have to walk through this nightmare with me.

At that moment my emotions were running all over the place and I couldn't shield her. I was hurting so bad and I needed to unleash my emotions on someone. I could tell she was fighting back tears. She was trying to be strong for me. I said, "Mom, I've been fighting for him, I don't know if I have anything left in me." My mom said, "Cassie. give this to God. You are going to have to let go and hand McGwire over to God." I said, "I can't mom, I can't let go. I have to keep holding on. I am his mother and I will never let go of him. I love him too much. I'm the one who has to fix this. I've prayed to God over and over and nothing has changed. Praying isn't working, nothing is working. I don't have any choice but to fight. I'm fighting alone and I'm tired, but I won't stop fighting for my son, no matter what it does to me. Nothing can stop me from finding my son again. He's lost, but I know he's still in there, I just have to find him again."

My mom said, "Cassie, quit fighting so hard and give in to God, let Him have this. It's not yours to keep, this isn't your battle, it's God's. You have to let go so God can work. Let Him fight for you." My mom started crying and I cried louder. I said, "I give up, I'm done." I was leaning against the wall and I slowly slid down the wall and hung the phone up. I was too weak to keep talking and I had to get off the phone, I had no more fight in me.

I was lost and hurt. I couldn't control my crying. I let everything out. Larkin was playing with his toys and I felt like a terrible Mom. I had a child I could take care of, that needed me, but I couldn't do anything. I was paralyzed against the wall. I couldn't focus, I wanted to give up and never move again. I tucked my head down and cried harder and harder then suddenly Larkin walked over to me and stood there looking at me.

He stooped down to my level and I looked up at him and he said, "Momma." I wiped my tears as they streamed down my face and said, "Hey baby and come see Momma" and I drew him close and sat him on my lap and hugged him as tight as I could and we sat there as I continued to cry. Larkin comforted me at that moment. I couldn't give up because Larkin needed me and deep down McGwire did too. I couldn't stop fighting. In that moment Larkin gave me strength that I didn't have. He gave me the will to get back up again, to rise out of this and keep going. He reminded me that day that our story wasn't over yet, it was only beginning.

# CHAPTER 27

# Did You Ask?

L et's pause here for a second before we go any further down this road. At this point in our story my relationship with God was not established yet. I knew to pray to God but I felt like praying was not the answer. I was praying, but did I ask? I was saying a prayer, but was I talking to God like I would to a friend? Was I being specific with Him? We need to ask God for what we need. It's not selfish to do that. God knows what's best for us, so asking Him for help guides us in the right direction.

Lately I have been working on this book a lot and trying to get it done in time for you to read. I have been really tired and just drained. I've been working a lot and life has gotten very busy and I knew I needed to rest. I have prayed about it and asked God if He wanted me to rest and I believe He did. If we ask, He listens and when we listen He blesses us. I had a week of rest and have used the week to get other jobs done that I haven't been able to do. My boys are such hard workers and they were helping me clean up the woods. Larkin is six years old now and McGwire is now thirteen. As you know Larkin is my ornery boy. He is the one that gets into everything. He is so curious all the time.

I have been on him a lot lately about asking permission to do things before he does them. He is really bad about doing something and not asking first and it can get him into trouble. We recently made some trails in our woods and I was walking down the trail. Out of the corner of my eye I saw a small car tire go rolling by. We had some old car tires laying in the woods that we were cleaning up and I realized Larkin had picked it up and it went rolling out of control. He couldn't stop it. I chased after it but couldn't stop it from rolling and there it went deep down into the woods. I looked back at Larkin and said, "Did you ask?" He shook his head ashamedly and said, "No."

I've been trying to get him to understand that he needs to ask before he does things because I know the consequences and he doesn't. I had to hike deep down into the woods into the valley to get that tire. I had to cross through thorn bushes and poison ivy, which I am very allergic to. At first I couldn't find the tire. It was lost somewhere in the woods. When I finally saw it, and started to go get it I realized my dog Jazz was down there with me. She is so prone to drift when we are down in the woods. As I was fighting my way to get to the tire through all the thorns and poison ivy, I looked up and Jazz was gone.

At this point I had another problem to deal with. I had to stop everything and look for her. My kids came down at the edge of the trail hollering for me to see what the hold up was. They asked if they could come down and help and I said "No, it's too steep for you guys, I don't want you to stumble and fall." When I finally found Jazz, I called her back to me and started to go back up with the tire. Then I realized I was trapped in an old fence.

I was frustrated because I needed to find a new path to get back up the hill. As I went through more thorns and poison ivy with the weight of the tire on my shoulders, McGwire noticed I was struggling, and before I knew it Mcgiwre was there guiding me on a new path. He met me halfway and said, "Mom, I'll take the tire and carry it for you, just follow me. This path has no thorns or poison ivy and it's not as steep." I followed McGwire and he led me safely to the top of the hill. My point to this story is God will meet you halfway too. When God sees you struggling, He will meet you where you are, just like McGwire met me. But you need to ask Him for what you need before you go and do it yourself. This is exactly why we need to ask God.

When McGwire was sick, I spent a lot of time at first refusing to bring my problems to the feet of Jesus and give them to him. I don't know why I waited so long. I guess I can't answer that question right now, but maybe that's where you are right now. You aren't ready to give it to God. God is so big and I didn't realize at the time He was bigger than the problem we were up against . At first I didn't ask for help, I just did what I felt like I needed to do with no direction but my own.

The path I took at first was like the struggle I went through to chase the tire. I ended up in the valley when McGwire was sick. I was constantly struggling and stumbling and it left me fighting through thorns and poison ivy. I was in the wilderness all alone struggling to stand on two feet, but God met me halfway when I finally gave in and asked for help. He picked me up and showed me the new path I needed to take. He carried the weight for me so I could find myself back on the mountain top.

Don't fight a fight that isn't yours to fight. God wants to fight for you. God allows us into the valley so we can learn to be dependent on Him. He leads us back up to the mountaintops too and that's where we find our breakthrough, but first we need to make our way through the wilderness and that's where Satan lives and tries to test us. We can only remain strong if we ask for guidance or we may end up back on that thorny path.

If Larkin asked me if he could pick up that tire I would have said, "No, it may roll down the hill." How do I know? Because this happened to me before, with something harder, an old tractor tire. If you think that car tire was bad, try getting an old tractor tire out of the woods. When I finally reached the top of our trails, I sat down exhausted and I had to laugh and Larkin looked at me thinking he was going to get a lecture. I looked at him and said, "Did you learn your lesson bud? Now do you know why we need to ask before we do something? Did you see all the problems mommy had because you didn't ask? Mommy isn't being mean to you, I just don't want anything bad to happen to you."

We all know how it is to be a parent and how we want our kids to bring their problems to us. As parents, we want our children to ask us for advice and we want to guide them. God is the same way, He wants us to ask first. If you ask you shall receive. I looked at Larkin and said, "Well bud, one good thing out of this is, you helped me add a new chapter in my book." He smiled and said, "See mommy I helped you with your Bible." That's what Larkin calls my book. He thinks when he wakes up in the morning and sees me typing on my computer, that I am writing the Bible.

My point in telling this is, we need to ask God for guidance and

He will lead us on the right path and you will avoid all the thorns and poison ivy.

# CHAPTER 28

# I'm Tired

I know you are reading this book right now and you're probably tired. I think everyone struggles with being tired. Life is so busy and we don't get enough sleep sometimes but when you're fighting a battle like I was, you become tired in a different way, a deeper kind of tired. I was so tired of waking up to the chaos or absence of McGwire. I had a hard time finding the strength to get up everyday, but Larkin was there to give me a reason to rise out of it. God will always supply us with the right people or the right weapons we need to fight back with.

Larkin helped me even when I didn't want to fight for it anymore. God is our strength and He will give us all the things we need to fight a battle, but He doesn't do the work for us. You have to make a choice. Do you let the battles consume you and let the enemy win? Or do you keep fighting even when you feel too tired? My advice is: don't give up when you're almost there. You can't stop short of the victory God has for you. Some of the most defining moments in life are done when people are tired.

There are some things in life we shouldn't do when we're tired, but when you are fighting the fight of your life, or in my case, fighting for my son. I was fighting while exhausted. Giving up wasn't a choice because I would have been giving up on McGwire. I needed God's strength, I needed to find God's power. I knew what I needed to do and that was to surrender to Him, but I was wearing myself out fighting a fight I shouldn't have fought. I don't know why I refused to surrender, but I guess I wasn't ready yet. I needed to get out of the darkness and lay all my fears at the feet of Jesus. I needed to hand them over so I could start over and quit fighting God and let Him fight for me and my family. When McGwire was sick, I fought everything that had to do with God.

My mom was constantly telling me to turn everything over to Him. She kept sending me sermons to my phone to listen to on my runs. I told her I would listen to them sometime but I never did. I couldn't wrap my head around turning everything over to someone I couldn't even see. God was invisible to me so why would I turn everything over to Him when I don't even know if He's there? I tried praying to God and felt like that wasn't working so I didn't trust Him. It was hard to trust in God when I never really went through anything this big before. I hadn't seen His power yet. What else could I do? I thought to myself, what does Mom want me to do, just sit back and let God do everything? How could I trust God would take it out of my hands? This was my son's life we're talking about, I couldn't trust anyone but myself. I was McGwire's mom and I couldn't let go.

Maybe this is how you feel too and it's ok. I think at some point of forming a relationship with God these thoughts may surface. Today I often look back and wonder why it took so long for me to give in. Why did I fight turning things over to Him? I wasted so much time and energy fighting something that I didn't need to fight. It didn't have to be so hard but I made it that way. The funny part about all this is, I told my mom I prayed but God wasn't answering my prayers so why would I turn my children over to Him.

Sometimes God is answering our prayers but we don't realize it. We often think God isn't working but in reality He is working and some of the answers to our prayers are right in front of us. The answers to my prayers were on my phone. God was answering my prayers by using my Mom. She sent me sermon after sermon and all I needed to do was push play, but I refused. Everytime I went for a run I had the opportunity to change our circumstances. I was delaying the process. We would have been out of this battle sooner if I would have just pushed play. It was something so simple but yet I made it out to be so hard.

God is such a good Father because He knew the perfect way to get through to me was through my passion for running. God knew my form of worship would be when I was on the move. He was moving towards me but I was running away from Him. He was trying to answer my prayers in a way that He knew would catch my attention. I was blinded by the storm my family was up against.

Let me warn you about something, Satan is very clever. He is so good at blindsiding you. He will hit you with something when you least expect it and his goal is to make you feel weak. He wants you to meditate on the bad things happening so you miss the good things that God is sending you. One of the biggest strategies Satan will use against you is, you have time. If he convinces you that you have time, it will prolong the process and it gives Satan time to continue to corrupt your mind. I told my mom I would eventually listen to one of those sermons. Days passed and I thought about listening to one but didn't do it. Satan convinced me that I could do it later. It was always later, but time was getting away from me and I needed to surrender to God and I needed to do it soon because things were getting worse.

God was making it easy for me but yet I continued to push Him away. The crazy thing about all this is, I was pushing God away just like McGwire was pushing me away. I was hurting God just like McGwire was hurting me. Now that I think about it, why did I do that? God was just trying to help me. He was just trying to get through to me but I fought Him and I was mad at Him. I was so angry at Him for not answering my prayers. He was, I just wasn't listening. I was doubting Him and I thought He had given up on my family but He hadn't. He already answered my prayers but I was too stubborn to listen.

Sometimes we have to put our guard down and let people help us. There are a lot of times God will use people to help us but if we keep pushing them away then we will never escape the battle we are in and Satan is counting on that. The time is ticking and we have a choice to make. Do we listen to Satan? Has he convinced you that you have time? Is he making you feel weak? Or do we listen to God? Do we believe He is going to help us through the battle? Maybe you feel weak right now, maybe you feel broken and vulnerable. These are the moments Satan will try to hit us hard but what he doesn't understand is that in the moments of our weaknesses are the moments God steps in and gives us His strength.

Just because you feel weak doesn't mean you can't win this battle.

You will win but you have to give in and let God help you fight. That
is where God likes us to be because that is where the transformation
begins. That is where we wake up and finally see how good God truly
is. I didn't figure out how good God was until I finally broke down
enough to pull up one of the sermons my mom sent me and I finally
gave in and pushed play.

Making the first step is so difficult but it may be the answer to
your prayers. The day I took the first step was because I was running
out of options. I was nearly at the end of myself. I decided to go for
a run to clear my head. I was about to pick a song to listen to but I
noticed my mom messaged me and I and looked at it. It was another
sermon, I shook my head. I backed out of my phone and something
nudged me to pull that message back up and I refused. I played my
song and began running.

As I ran something nudged me again to pull that message up
and I ignored it. I thought to myself I need to listen to one of the
sermons just to pacify mom, but then I thought what's the point. I
won't understand what they're talking about and it will make my
run boring. I continued to run and listen to my music and something
nudged me harder. I thought of my Mom begging me to listen to one
of the sermons, then suddenly I thought of McGwire and how sick he
was. My chest became heavy and my music felt dull. I wasn't enjoying
the music so I stopped and pulled up my moms message and I thought
fine, I will listen to one and then maybe mom will stop sending them
to me. I pushed play and the sermon began and I started running.

As I ran, I listened. I began thinking, this isn't for me, I felt weird
listening to it. I let it play a little longer trying to give it a chance. I
just wasn't absorbing it so I was about to stop and change it back to
my music until suddenly the preacher said something that hit me. He
said the same thing my mom has been telling me this whole time. He
said, "You need to hand your children over to God. You need to drop
to your knees and surrender. Tell God you are tired and you can't do
it anymore. Confess everything to Him and let go of it and let Him
take it." I continued to listen to the sermon and I got through all of it.

When I got home I sat down and took it all in. I felt different
than usual after a run. I decided to take a shower and I thought about

everything I'd heard. The sermon was stuck in my head. The sermon must have gotten through to me a little bit, but I still had my doubts it would work. I had already asked for help, I had already prayed, but maybe I did need to drop to my knees.

I was scared of all of this. I had nothing left and knew this was the only thing left that I hadn't done. I just wanted someone to help my son. I couldn't trust God was the answer because I didn't know Him and He was still invisible to me. I needed Mom to fix this, I trusted her because she was my mom. I needed a visible person to fix this. I needed a doctor, someone, anyone. They needed to be seen by me not hiding in a Bible verse somewhere.

I was determined my son wasn't going to lose this battle. We were going to win, but I needed a new strategy and that's what the runs did for me. This run was different though, my new strategy involved God this time. Running was therapy for me, but I never invited God into it. I did that day. That was the day I met God. I mean really met Him. It was the first day I invited God to run with me or maybe He invited me to run with Him and I finally broke down and said yes. I still didn't trust God yet, but I was getting there.

I relied too much on my mom to help me fix this and too much on myself, not God. Mom knew she couldn't help me. She knew this was out of her hands and Whose hands it needed to be in. She knew this wasn't her battle to fight and she knew it wasn't mine either. My mom saw me shutting down and getting tired from the battle. I was struggling and she knew Who could help. Mom had an understanding about God that I was unfamiliar with, she knew God, but I didn't. She knew the sermons were the answer. God used my Mom to help me because He knew eventually I would listen to her.

God was answering my prayers. He sent me on a run and He sent me a sermon, but it was up to me to make the choice to listen to it. God gave me a way but I had to do the work to get to the next step. I finally gave in. I may have been headed to somewhere unfamiliar but this was the place God intended me to go. After getting dressed I sat down and thought about everything. I remembered we had a Bible my mom gave me that I had shoved in some old chest. I decided to dig it out. I sat back down on my bed and was very hesitant about opening it. It scared me for some reason. I slowly opened it to a random page and began to read. I struggled reading it because it wasn't making any sense to me so I closed it. I was going to put it back in the old chest but something stopped me.

I thought about it and decided to take it upstairs to McGwire's room and put it on his nightstand. I believe that day represented a little faith, because I thought maybe if I can't read it, maybe if it's sitting in his room that will be enough to help him, even if we don't read it. God was about to do something so big and so powerful but first I needed to do something. I needed to fall down on my knees and surrender.

# CHAPTER 29

# I Surrender

As a mother handing your child to someone else is hard because you want to be the one to protect them and take care of them but it was out of my control. I needed Jesus to take over. It's ok to be scared, but don't let fear take over. Fear can ride with you but don't let it drive.

I was a mother who felt the weight of the world on her shoulders. I felt it was up to me to take care of everyone. I always put myself on the back burner because I felt everyone was my responsibility. This is a good quality to have, but we can't do it all. We need to let others help us and we need to let God take the weight off of our shoulders. As much as I knew I needed help, I continued to try to do it on my own. I've never been a quitter and felt like surrendering was giving up.

Now looking back, I don't think it was quitting that kept me from surrendering. I wasn't ready to let go. A lot of people are in my situation and the only thing that keeps them from surrendering is letting go. We control our own lives because we feel we know best, but in reality if we control everything we will take ourselves down a dead end road. I believe we're not ready to let go of the things of this world but what we don't understand is we are letting go of things that we never had control of in the first place and we're picking up so much more when we let go.

God has so much more to offer but we have to surrender to find out what He has for us. I'm not good at letting go of people or things I love. My mom says, anything I do I get too involved with it and follow it through until the end no matter what it does to me in the process. Mom was constantly telling me to turn my children over to God and I believe she was planting a seed when she did. When I finally broke down and listened to that sermon, the seed planted was being watered. It took one more battle to get to the very end of myself and that was what made the seed grow.

On the day I surrendered, I had no intentions to do so. I was having a really bad morning with McGwire. Nothing was going right. He woke up mean, as usual. He didn't want to go to school and didn't want to eat the breakfast I offered him. He said I was being mean for making him go to school, but he didn't want to stay home with me either. He didn't like the clothes I picked out for him and he didn't want me to brush his hair. He didn't do his homework the night before because he fought it for three hours so we left it blank. He didn't want to leave it blank because he knew he would get into trouble. Everything was wrong according to him and everything was a big struggle that morning.

I was so tired of fighting with him. I felt bad, but I wanted him out the door and I wanted him to go to school. At the same time I didn't want him to leave on bad terms. I wanted to make up and give him a big hug, but he wouldn't let me. I hated leaving the house with anything unresolved. The bus arrived early and he didn't have his shoes on so I gestured for the bus to wait. McGwire took his time getting his shoes on.

As he walked out the door I watched him walk down the driveway taking his time to get on the bus as it waited for him. I felt sad when he left. I wanted him back home, but I knew if he was here it would be a huge fight. I was relieved the chaos road off in the bus so my youngest could be rid of the destruction McGwire was creating that morning. Now we could have peace. At the same time, I wanted McGwire here with us too. I was lost in my thoughts and wanted to hold Larkin but he was ready to play and I didn't have it in me to sit down and play with him. I hated that, but I couldn't focus, my head was cluttered and my chest was so heavy.

I was tired of this being my everyday norm. I wanted my old life back, I wanted McGwire to be the boy I once knew. I wanted my family back, but unfortunately this was our new reality and I was over it. Larkin and I headed upstairs to McGwire's room to make the bed. I struggled making the bed, I didn't have any energy left in me. I sat down on the edge of the bed and lifted Larkin up on the bed with me and laid him beside me.

As I layed there, I tried so hard to fight back the tears, but I couldn't. I wanted to be strong for Larkin but I couldn't anymore. I looked into Larkin's chocolate brown eyes and whispered, "Mommy loves you baby." He touched my wet cheeks as if he was wiping the tears away. I was lost and had nothing left in me. I had endured the pain way too long, and couldn't do it anymore. We had a cross hanging on the wall that my Aunt Judy bought for the kids. I walked over to the cross and placed my hand on it.

I was so tired, weak and weary I couldn't go on like this and I knew it. I couldn't do it anymore, but as a mother those words are hard to say. I whispered, "God, I give up." I couldn't believe those words came from my mouth. I felt defeated as if I had lost the battle. I began to cry out to God. "God, I can't do it anymore." My legs started to tremble and I dropped to my knees and sobbed uncontrollably, "God I need your help. I need you to take this from me. I don't have the strength for it anymore. My son is lost, I'm lost, my family is broken. I tried to put the pieces back together but I couldn't. I hand my children over to You. I surrender."

Tears were streaming from my eyes but suddenly I had a sense of peace and looked up and saw the Bible I had put on McGwire's night stand. I walked over and opened it to a random page and began reading. As I read it was as if the author spoke the words that I felt. They pierced me and I cried as I read the words out loud. It was Psalms 143 in the Christian Standard Bible.

It said, "Lord, hear my prayer. In your faithfulness listen to my plea, and in your righteousness answer me. Do not bring your servant into judgment, for no one alive is righteous in your sight. For the enemy has pursued me, crushing me into the ground, making me live in darkness like those long dead. My spirit is weak within me; my heart is overcome with dismay. I remember the days of old; I meditate on all you have done; I reflect on the work of your hands. I spread out my hands to you; I am like a parched land before you. Answer me quickly, Lord; my spirit fails. Don't hide your face from me, or I will be like those going down to the Pit. Let me experience your faithful love in the morning, for I trust in you. Reveal to me the way I should go because I appeal to you. Rescue me from my enemies, Lord; I come to you for protection. Teach me to do your will, for you are my God. May your gracious spirit lead me on level ground. For your name's sake, Lord, let me live. In your righteousness, deliver me from trouble, and in your faithful love destroy my enemies. Wipe out all those who attack me, for I am your servant."

After reading those words I felt some kind of relief. I still felt sad but there was a sense of peace that came over me. I marked the page and layed back down with Larkin. Sometimes in this world we are taught to fight for everything we have, but In God's eyes, it's about surrendering everything to Him. We have to lay everything at Jesus's feet and pick up our cross and carry it, moving forward to the path God is leading us. That was the day I finally let go and surrendered to God and that's when things were about to change.

# CHAPTER 30

# I Believe, But God, Help Me Believe

After I surrendered to God, it wasn't like everything changed right away. It's a process. It's a process that we have to trust. It doesn't happen overnight. You have to take the steps God is leading you to, and go with it and trust that He is leading you in the right way. My mom found a doctor that specializes in children with OCD, autism, and recently PANDAS. I watched a video on this doctor and he explained what PANDAS was and he had a short clip of a mother who talked about her son with PANDAS. She explained that it was as if he changed overnight just like McGwire did.

The boy reminded me of McGwire. He was very active in sports. He was also a very kind, loving child. Things changed rapidly after he developed strep throat. I was intrigued by this. It felt good to find another mother that was battling the same storm. I could relate to her in many ways. I could see in her eyes how hard this was for her when she explained it. She ended the video by saying there was hope. I needed to hear those words.

She said this doctor saved her son and he was finally back to his normal self. She said, "It was a process but it was worth every step." I knew at that very moment I needed to make an appointment with this doctor. I found the number for the doctor's office and called to see if I could get McGwire in to see that particular doctor.

I talked to the receptionist and she reassured me we were coming to the right place. She explained to me what PANDAS was and asked me about McGwire's symptoms. She told me I wasn't alone in this. She assured me that McGwire could get help and could fight this and they would help us too. The only problem was the office did not accept insurance and it was very expensive. I was scared. I didn't know if we could afford it so I told her I would discuss it with my husband and call her back.

I got off the phone with mixed emotions. I knew in my heart this was the right place for McGwire. It was the answer we were searching for. I had hope, but could we afford it? I began to cry and pray.

I said, "God is this where I need to take McGwire? I need help believing this is actually going to work?" After surrendering to Him I was finally seeing some evidence of a breakthrough but I had to learn to trust Him even when I had doubts. It's hard to believe something is going to work when you have a new set of fears. We were back to worrying about our finances. I finally surrendered to God and things changed, but I was expecting everything to be better all at once. Isn't that how it's supposed to work? No, unfortunately not.

I had hoped this was the answer to my prayers, but we also had a new challenge and we were back to making a new decision. I was beginning to believe in God more, but I needed Him to help with my unbelief, my doubts and fears. What if this isn't the answer and we get to the point we are broke financially and McGwire still doesn't get better? Then what do we do? Where do we go from there? The problem is when we doubt something we convince ourselves that we don't believe that God will come through.

When you first develop a relationship with God you begin to trust Him a little, but you still have a little doubt because you haven't seen His full power yet so you still need guidance from Him. We still believe in God, but when we are in the middle of our battle, and things are going up and down and back and forth, it makes us question things. I knew McGwire needed to see this doctor, but how could he? Maybe if I was still working as a mammographer, but I wasn't. I was barely making money with my classes. How would we afford this doctor when we were already struggling as it was?

I was doubting everything. Why did it have to be so hard? We finally got an answer to our prayers, but now this. The thing is, you are going to run into some moments where you have to make some hard decisions that will test your faith, but you will find the blessing underneath your doubts. You have to invite Jesus into the root of your problems and He will work you through them. Your faith grows when you walk through your doubts.

I felt like I needed a new plan but I knew deep down in my heart that this was the new plan and I needed to work into it trusting that we wouldn't fall behind financially. Using your skills and abilities to plan something out is ok, but your skills and abilities will eventually fail you, but God never will. You will need God in these kinds of moments. He will guide you and walk with you through things that look and seem bigger than you.

Sometimes it's better not to look at the situation and evaluate it. Sometimes it's best to trust and walk through it. When you think, I can't do this, switch your way of thinking and tell yourself you can. Sometimes we get so caught up in the chaos we are walking into that we often forget Who we are walking with. God is with you through it all and if you are doubting, you just have to trust God will lead you the whole way there. God is so much bigger than your problem. Don't downsize what He can do. He can take a situation that looks impossible and turn it around and make it your blessing. When God shows His power, it will be bigger than you can imagine.

When you finally see His power in a big way then that's when you start establishing trust in Him. That is when your faith grows. We have to start walking into the things we are scared of. Every step we make towards something bigger than us, we are getting stronger. We have to remember everything is done in God's perfect timing and I knew the time was now. I needed to make that appointment now and trust we would make it. I needed to decrease so God could increase. I needed to stop thinking and just do it. This could be the answer to my prayers.

McGwire could get better and that was enough for me to make the appointment. I could find a million reasons why I shouldn't make the appointment, but I picked up the phone without discussing it with my husband and made the appointment anyway. I would rather go broke and live on the streets than see my son living in this torment. I didn't care what it cost me, his life was worth so much more than money. This wasn't about money, this was about my son's life. The next challenge we faced was McGwire wasn't going to be able to see the main doctor for six months so the other option was for him to see the nurse practitioner, but I didn't care. I just wanted to be in that office. It was going to be a month before we could be seen. I knew it was going to be a long time, but God gave me the strength that day to fight and endure the wait.

# Fighting Back

I had to find a way to keep fighting. This was going to be a long, hard month so I needed to be equipped with the right weapons to fight back. One thing to keep in mind is that there's a real enemy out there and he is trying to wear you down and make you too tired to fight back. Keep fighting anyway. My advice is to not let the enemy steal from you what is yours. Waiting a whole month to see the doctor was hard because McGwire was getting worse everyday. I knew I couldn't wait until I was feeling one hundred percent to fight back or I would never get back what was stolen from me. I wasn't going to leave McGwire vulnerable and unprotected. I was his mom and absolutely no one was going to take what was mine.

In NLT Matthew 16:23, "Jesus turned to Peter and said, Get away from me, Satan! You are a dangerous trap to me. You are seeing things merely from a human point of view, not from God's." We can't let Satan get in the way of the purpose God is leading us towards. We have to fight back but we need to find the right weapons.

What are your weapons? Running is one of the weapons. My most current weapons were the sermons sent to me by my mother. Sometimes you have to merge your weapons together to make them stronger. I had both weapons to use but I needed to learn how to use them for my strength.

When I merged my runs and the sermons together it made my running more powerful, more meaningful. My running became my classroom. I began listening to them on a regular basis. I asked mom to send me new ones. I didn't like them at first but after a while I saw the transformation in me. I was growing in my faith. I started learning about God and who He truly was. I was finally understanding His power. I began to be more dependent on His strength and less dependent on my own.

Running was my hobby, but pairing it with the sermons took it to a whole new level. One day I decided to go for a run at Paradise. It was mid morning and the sun was shining so bright. It was chilly, but a nice day. My husband let me escape for a little bit. I placed my earbuds in and started listening to one of the sermons.

There was a pasture of cows in the field beside the road. I don't always pay attention to them but on this day they caught my attention. Out of the corner of my eye, when I started running, I noticed one of the cows running along side of me on the other side of the fence. I smiled, and thought this was kind of cool. It started with one cow then it was two. Suddenly another cow joined in and before long I had about seven or eight of them jogging by my side.

I noticed their pace started to pick up so I picked up my pace too. I was loving this. I looked over at them and smiled and they looked at me and we kept going. Suddenly they were going even faster than before. I was starting to get a slight twinge in my stomach from running so fast. Next they came to a dead stop. I stopped too and began to laugh. I realized what the cows were doing.

I thought this whole time God was creating a special moment for me by running with the cows, but that's not at all what was happening. I noticed where they stopped, there were about ten to twelve young calves standing there unattended. When they saw me running they realized their babies had no one there to protect them. They thought I was after their babies. They saw me as a threat or an enemy and they were not going to let the enemy steal what was theirs. Those mothers were going to fight so they could protect their babies.

My point is, we have to fight when we see the enemy coming in for the attack. First we have to find the weapons to use to fight back. The cows knew that their babies were vulnerable and nothing was there to protect them, so they fought back by running the race of their lives to get to their babies before something got to them first. Don't let the enemy steal what is yours and if he does, you have to use the weapons that you are equipped with and link it to God's strength and fight back.

Don't give up when you are tired, keep running until you get there so nothing can come between you and what you are fighting for. God is your weapon, He is your strength and bent knees are the surrender it takes to unlock the power you need to be able to fight. Try to find an outlet, something that you love to do and link it with God's power and that will be one of the weapons you need in your battle. Another weapon I used was the power of the pen.

I'm going to be completely honest, this book you're reading right now wasn't intended to be a book. It originally started as a journal. A lot of the pieces I wrote in this book were pulled straight from my journal. When McGwire was so sick I began journaling.

I can remember one night after struggling to get him to go to sleep. I came downstairs and on my countertop was a journal my mom bought me. She told me to write in it when I felt like I needed to release my emotions. It wasn't easy for me to talk to people about all of this so I used the journal as a way to do that. I began writing one night and it became an every night routine. It felt good to release everything I had trapped inside of me.

These were raw emotions that I had running deep inside of me through the midst of my family's storm. Sometimes I would write for hours and not realize it. I had so much to say and after writing these deep painful words, I felt better. I knew I needed to talk to a person too, but I couldn't bring myself to express my emotions to an actual person. Sometimes I didn't have the energy to talk about it, so I would write instead.

Little did I know when I stayed up late at night and wrote on those tear covered pieces of paper, I was slowly transforming it into a book. That's how God works. He uses our scars and makes a blessing out of them. One day when I pulled out the old journal entries, I read them and they cut me like a knife. That was the day I knew I needed to make the old journal entries into a book. I sat down every morning and took each journal entry and typed them into my computer, but I kept hitting dead ends.

There were times I would stare at my computer at a loss for words. I didn't know what to say, but my breaking point was always in the parts of the story that were hard for me to write. Talking about

McGwire's sickness was too much for me sometimes. It was too raw and it made me cry, so I would stop. I found myself rushing through this book wanting it to be finished because it hurt so much reliving all the pain again. I began to put a deadline on it thinking I would be finished with it by now. It felt like it was one hundred miles away from being done. I knew I couldn't rush through something like this or the story wouldn't be right. The message God intended on me giving wouldn't be fulfilled.

To be honest, at times writing this book put so much anxiety in me that I found myself making excuses not to write. I got to the point I slammed the laptop shut and never opened it again, not until something compelled me to pick it back up. I believe it was you and your need for this book that always pulled me back to it. I know you are struggling right now like I was and that is what kept me gravitating towards it. There was something about it that never let me completely quit writing. I knew I needed to pick up that pen and write again.

When I eventually picked it back up and I hit the rough spots in the book, I would come to a screeching stop. I tried writing this book three different times and the last time I shut it, I didn't open it back up again for another year. On New Year's Eve, my family and I wrote a list of things we wanted to accomplish for that year and I wrote that I was going to finish this book. It didn't happen. I have written that for the last five years and I kept carrying it over to the next list. I thought to myself, not this time, I am going to do this. I'm not stopping this time. I knew it was time to write again.

The next day I opened my laptop again. When I opened it and placed my flash drive in everything was gone. I had lost all of it. I was devastated. I wanted to give up but I said no, not this time. I can do this. I will start all over. If God wants you to do something, there will always be something that will get in your way trying to stop you.

Satan obviously didn't want this to happen. If bad things are happening to you, then this means Satan is trying to stop you. This is a good way of knowing that you have to do this. This is your purpose because Satan wouldn't be trying to stop you. He sees you as a threat. Satan will do everything in his power to prevent this from happening, but don't let him. There are ways around everything, and Jesus is the way.

Don't believe Satan's lies and don't let him convince you otherwise. I was so upset but something told me to start over, don't give up. You can make it better. I started over and today I am still writing. I'm not giving up on you, either. I have to keep going and trust the process. The chapters must go on; the journey will continue; the story has to go on, it isn't over yet, our testimony is for you.

CHAPTER 32

# Fear

I'm scared. My fears have taken over and I'm in a bad place right now. A place I have never been before but now that I'm here, I feel stuck and honestly I don't know how to get back or how to move forward. I'm in a pit and I need help getting out. I need help God, where are you? This was one of my journal entries I wrote while McGwire was sick.

As I read it now, I remember the feeling so vividly. I was in a lonely place then, but here I stand today. I rose up from the situation and now I'm here telling you that you will rise from it too. When I wrote this, my thoughts were in a dark place. Journaling was good for me because I was able to express how I felt at the time and as you read it, you can tell I was scared and lost.

Today I can write to you to say it's going to be ok, you can overcome your storm. Back then, when I was in the midst of my storm, I wouldn't have been able to say that. At that time I would have told you it was the end and there was no way out. My way of thinking back then was blurred by what I was dealing with. Why can I stand here today telling you that you will rise up from all this, but back then I couldn't?

The difference between then and now is fear. Fear is a strong emotion that causes us to look too far into the future and a lot of times we think the worst. In most cases, the thing we worry so much about doesn't even happen, but it's the fact that we don't know that scares us. There's a way to help you overcome your fears. It's called framing. Let me explain.

McGwire has been doing some catching in baseball this year. As I watched him catch, I started thinking that life is like being a catcher.

We need to look at things like a catcher does. McGwire used to be a catcher several years ago and this brought back some old memories watching him catch again. He knows when to take the risk of throwing the runners out. He stays very calm and throws it without thinking much about it. He also knows when to hold the ball to save his team from making mistakes and letting the opposing team take the lead. McGwire is good at framing the ball.

Framing the ball simply means to receive a pitch in a way that makes it more likely for an umpire to call it a strike. This is an art a catcher needs to learn. It gives the umpire the illusion that the ball crosses the plate as a strike when it actually is a little off to the side of the plate. McGwire loves to frame the ball. He practices it a lot. The more the catcher practices, the better the frame looks. Even if it's not a strike, it will look like one.

I think this is such a clever idea in baseball, but what if you apply it to your life spiritually? If we did this, I believe our lives would be a whole new ball game. We need to learn how to frame the ball when we face fear. What I mean is, when we look at life from one point of view, our outcomes look bad, but what if we frame it. What if we fake it? I don't mean cover it up. I mean what if we change our way of thinking? What if we say things like, we're going to make it through this, or I feel weak but I know Who will make me stronger.

We have to stop saying things like, we'll never make it through this, we will never get better. What if we say, I'm scared, but I trust you God that You will lead me through this. We have to learn to change our way of thinking. We have to learn to look on the bright side and that's easier said than done. I also know some situations are worse than others, but try to stay positive through the midst of your storm, because if your spirits are good, your outcome will look better. We are so good at twisting things to look bad. Why don't we try twisting and turning things in another angle and try to make them look good? Let's make them look like strikes.

When McGwire was sick, nothing looked good. Things got worse before they got better. You have to practice framing and once you get good at it, maybe by faith the umpire will call a strike. We can't let the opposing team win the game, we have to take risks and not think about it even if we are weak, we can frame it to make us look strong. We also need to stop and hold the ball sometimes because we're not going to let Satan win the game. We will do anything it takes to win the game, even if we have to frame it. We need to fight back, we haven't lost the game yet but Satan wants you to think you have. He wants to get into your head so much that you give up.

My son is also a pitcher and he gets in his head so much when he is pitching. He gets discouraged when the other team hits the ball off of him. I tell him, "You are thinking about it all wrong. You are throwing strikes, that's why they are hitting it off of you. That's a good thing, not a bad thing. You are doing your job. That's why it's important to be a team."

Sometimes we throw strikes but we need people to back us up. Our lives are just like a simple baseball game. We get tired and we're scared and we want to know when the nightmare will be over. We want to know when God is going to help us make the breakthrough and we try to take steps before God wants us to. We need to operate on God's timeline, not ours.

As a batter, when you step up to the plate getting ready to hit, your hands are shaky, you're scared you're going to strike out. You need the win and it's all up to you. God wants you to swing the bat when He tells you to swing. If you keep swinging too early or too late, you might miss the ball or the breakthrough. Sometimes when we operate off of our timeline or swing the bat too early or too late, things don't always go in the right direction, it may go foul, then we end up on the wrong path and don't get anywhere.

God will help us fight for it. It's not over yet when you keep hitting a foul, but we need to slow down, take a deep breath in and reset ourselves. When we step back into the batter's box, we need to step into it with confidence, it's ok if we are scared but we need to trust God will tell us the right time to swing. We have to let the ball travel and when it's the right time, God will tell us when to swing, and then, exactly, right then, we'll make our breakthrough and we get our hit.

Our lives are just like a simple baseball game, we have to run through the bases and eventually we will find our way home. Framing is simply faith and maybe you don't have any faith yet because you haven't been through something like this before but if you keep walking your faith will grow with each step. We have to walk by faith not by sight. Fear will destroy us. Our minds can corrupt us. Fear of the unknown will sink us further and further into the pit. We find ourselves in a back and forth battle of what the next step is.

Where do we go from here? That's the question. How do we move forward when we don't even know where we are headed? We try to hold onto the things we feel are getting us through all this. We think those things are all we have left but sometimes those things are what God wants us to let go of. Sometimes we can't get our blessings until we put some things down. If you keep an open hand, God will fill it. When I prayed night after night, sometimes I wasn't sure if God even heard my prayers. Was He even listening? I had no evidence to support that God even heard my prayers. McGwire wasn't getting better. It didn't feel like God was working, it felt more like He was sleeping.

Maybe that's where you are today. You don't know what your next move is. When you pray about it, you don't feel like you get a clear answer from God. There will be times in your life where it will appear you're all alone, but in reality you're not because God is with you. There will be moments where you'll have open spaces between your prayers and God's deliverance. We don't know what to do in these open spaces so we get stuck in them. Fear takes over in these gaps. We develop feelings and emotions that cause us to react in the wrong way. We start doing things on our own because the spaces are too lonely.

Fear lives in these gaps, but it's in these gaps where we reach the next level. Fear diminishes our trust in God. In some cases I was at a loss for words to say to God. I didn't have the energy to speak to Him or even seek Him anymore. I was new at all of this. I didn't know scripture and didn't really know how to pray. I wasn't sure if I was doing it right. I knew I needed help. I was in a confined space that I needed out of.

What if I told you it doesn't matter how much you know about God, or how much you say to Him. Maybe the fall of collapsing to your knees is enough. Maybe your cry for help means something more than you will ever know. Maybe God hears your scream. Maybe you are in the dark but being in the dark makes it easier to see the light. Maybe you're scared but fear is all you need to make the next move. Maybe fear is what drives your faith. Maybe fear eliminates everything but God. Maybe fear will remove all those things standing in the way of your blessing.

Fear is what helps us see God more clearly. All you need is God and nothing else. He is your weapon to fight back and your strength to get up. God knows we are going to be scared sometimes. It takes being scared to open our eyes. It takes being in this dark place to finally see some light. If you feel you can't talk to God, just know He knows your thoughts and is thankful you called on Him. God wants you to come to Him and He will meet you where you are. When I'm at the lowest point in my life, in the darkest places, and completely at rock bottom, that's when I feel God the most.

You might think, I'm not good at praying and haven't been in church for years, and others are so much better at this than me, but that doesn't matter, God still loves you. Or you're thinking I don't know if I believe in God. Well you have to start somewhere and I'm here to tell you I started rough. I started rusty but God still heard me even when my thoughts were not positive. Your head doesn't have to be in the right place as long as your mouth is speaking the right name. Fear may be found in the gaps but God is too and it's the gap that takes you to the next chapter.

Today I praise God for what He did in my life but back then. I didn't know how to praise Him because fear took over. Today I have gratitude because I know God is good and I know what He has done for me. When a new problem hits and knocks me down again, I have a hard time praising God because fear takes over once more. The difference between then and now is I remember what God has done for me and I praise Him and I trust that He will do it again. If God did it for me back then, He will do it for me again. I may not understand what He is doing or why He's allowing another storm but I trust Him. It may feel like God isn't there but He's behind the scenes working on your next big thing. He's in that empty space that you want out of and He's clearing the way so you can come out of it with victory.

You can win this game but you have to fight back. Even if you are not throwing strikes, frame it, maybe by faith that the ball will become a strike.

# CHAPTER 33

# Beyblades

Everyday I woke up, I knew we were one day closer to McGwire's doctor's appointment. I was ready to go now but knew I had to count down the days to get through. McGwire woke up everyday ready to fight, he had his guard up and I never understood why. There was a war going on inside of him and he was scared so he stayed strong by being mean.

Deep down inside I think his anger covered up his fears and sorrow that was trapped inside. I know we all deal with mean people in our lives and we don't understand why they are so mean but I'm willing to bet it's a cover for something they're up against. Hurting people tends to hurt others. When we carry a lot of pain inside, sometimes we lash out at those we love the most because we feel most comfortable with them. I think when my son was at school or around other people, he had to hold in the torment inside of him. When he got home, I was an easy target. When he got home he felt like he could finally release all his pain to me, but it ended up with him hurting me and that was never his intention.

The guilt was eating him alive but instead of fixing it he ended up making it worse. It was a vicious cycle and it tormented him. He never wanted to hurt me but because he was hurting he didn't know how to control it because it controlled him. He had a battle going inside his head and he was constantly fighting it. We don't know what goes on behind closed doors. We don't know the kind of lives people battle when they get home. A lot of people wear masks to disguise their feelings. My son wore the mask of anger while I wore the mask of a fake smile. We both put up walls for protection from the war we were facing.

One day after folding laundry, I walked into the living room to see McGwire playing with one of his toys. This caught me by surprise because he hasn't played with his toys for a long time, he just laid around all the time. He was playing with a present my mom got him for Christmas. The toy he was playing with was called Beyblade Bursts.

Beyblades are like a spinning top. They came with an arena they could battle in. Several people could compete against each other. The object of the game was for you and your opponent(s) to launch your beyblades after a countdown of three and have your beyblade battle the other beyblade(s) to try and knock them out of the arena or until one stop. You gain more points if you burst the other beyblade(s). If you accomplish one of the three goals, you win.

As I watched him play with the beyblades, I stood there and soaked in the moment. As he launched his beyblade he watched it spin over and over. I stood very still and very quietly so I could watch him. I didn't want to interrupt this moment because I didn't know how long it would last. I finally gave in and walked into the living room and sat down on the floor beside him and said "Hey pal, what are you doing." He looked up at me and said "What does it look like I'm doing?" I said, "Looks like you're playing with your beyblades." He said "Yep." I said, "Can I play?" He looked at me and thought for a second, then said "I guess."

I didn't know how to launch my beyblade so I asked him how to do it. He quickly showed me and I launched it and I did terribly, McGwire looked at me and said "Wow you suck at this." I was angry at first when he said that but I didn't say anything because I didn't want to ruin the moment, so I agreed by smiling and saying "Yes I do." I kept trying and finally I got it. I said "Ok, are you ready to battle?" He said "Sure," so we battled, and of course he won. McGwire had mastered it and I was happy he won because I was scared that if I won the moment would be over and he would get angry.

After a few battles something must have gone off in McGwire because he suddenly got up and layed down on the couch. I said "What are you doing? Aren't we battling?" He said, "Nah, I don't want to anymore." I hated the moment was over but I was happy that

McGwire finally found something he was interested in doing, it gave me a little hope. I was finally able to get close to him and that was progress.

Later that evening while my husband and I were doing the dishes, I noticed McGwire was playing with his beyblades again. This made me so happy. I stopped what I was doing and walked into the living room and I said, "Hey bud, do you wanna battle again?" He looked at me and said, "Sure." As time went on the beyblades became his obsession but I didn't care because these toys were now his outlet. I needed to do this with him, this was my way to get in. So I spent hours playing beyblades with him, all my work was put to the side because I needed to do this for him. When I grew tired, I would tag my husband in and we would switch. One of us would play beyblades while one of us played with Larkin.

One day recently my husband and I were cleaning out the basement and I came across these old beyblades. They were all dusty because it's been years since my kids played with them. I sat down and cried as I held the arena in my hands. These beyblades carry a sentimental value to me because they helped McGwire through his journey of PANDAS. As I sat there I thought to myself, "Why were the beyblades so important to him?" Then it hit me.

McGwire used to sit and watch them spin and he would become mesmerized by them. Some of the beyblades were made for endurance but certain ones could spin for a long time and they won because they lasted the longest. Maybe watching the beyblades spin reminded McGwire of how he felt. He was so confused, lost and disoriented from his sickness. He probably felt like his life was spinning out of control too, but he knew he had to endure the spin to win the battle. Some beyblades would fly out of the arena because the impact of the collision against the other beyblade was too much for them. PANDAS came on strong and we never saw it coming. When McGwire took the hit, the impact was too much for him and it knocked him off his feet, just like the beyblades.

I believe the beyblades were important to McGwire because he was able to relate to them. The biggest comparison I see with the beyblades is the bursting aspect. It was a battle every time you launched your beyblade. You never knew what would happen, until you began to study them. McGwire studied the beyblades often and he began to know the strategy. To burst the beyblades, you had to discover where the other beyblades were vulnerable. You had to find their weak spots and hit them. When your beyblade hit the other beyblades weak spot, the other beyblade would break into pieces. You could always put the pieces back together but if your opponent knew where to hit you, you would burst everytime.

The beauty of all this is that the beyblades were interchangeable. What I mean by this is, if you have a lot of different beyblades, which we did, you could find different pieces that were stronger and not as vulnerable and you could create a stronger version of your favorite beyblade. Then when your opponent went against you, they had a harder time bursting you because you were stronger. You were equipped with new and improved armor.

God revealed something to me that I couldn't see until now. McGwire was sick and he was fighting a battle inside his head. Everyday he felt like he was spinning out of control. He knew he needed to endure it but he was feeling weak. He was fighting the battle of his life and the enemy was studying him. The enemy knew where McGwire was vulnerable and he found his weak spots and went in for the attack. He was slowly breaking apart piece by piece. He was shattered and desperately needed someone to put him back together. He needed a savior. When God comes in for the rescue, He will not put you back together with the same pieces you originally had because they are too weak.

God wants to strengthen you and create a better version of you, a stronger version. God will equip you with new and improved armor. McGwire needed stronger pieces, he needed new armor so he could get back up and face this war again. McGwire's sickness may have had a hold on him but maybe the beyblades gave him hope. By studying these beyblades, McGwire knew what it took to win the battle he was fighting. He learned that your weaknesses don't define you because you can strengthen them. God revealed this to McGwire through something so simple and small. These beyblades were the thing that finally got through to him.

God was giving McGwire a battle that he could finally win so he could take the knowledge of the battle with the beyblades and use it to fight for his life back. God was teaching him how to fight back in a way he could understand. My son was weary from the fight inside of him but with the beyblades he found his strength and he knew how to win. McGwire was scared in his own battle but he found confidence in the battle of his beyblades. As long as he was playing beyblades he was winning and he never wanted to stop because he needed the win. He knew the fight wasn't over yet.

I spent hours launching beyblades and began to grow tired of launching one after another but I stayed and played with McGwire because I knew deep down inside my heart I needed to. Something told me to do this with McGwire. The beyblades were the push McGwire needed to rise out of the sickness he was fighting. God was preparing us how to fight back through a simple toy. God doesn't always come out in big ways like we think He does. Sometimes we can find God in the smallest places. Don't give up, keep fighting because you are getting stronger, just stay close to God and put that new armor on because you will win this battle and come out with victory.

# CHAPTER 34

# Hiding From The Enemy's Attack

hy do we take cover? Why do we hide? I've found out the enemy attacks us because he sees us as a threat. He wouldn't be going after us if he wasn't scared. He sees potential in us and wants to stop us before the blessing happens. If you're struggling right now, it's because something amazing is about to happen. I often wondered why my son hid all the time.

He was constantly hiding from me, and it scared me because I couldn't find him. Kids with PANDAS hide, it's one of the symptoms. I never understood why he hid, but thinking about it now I feel like he hid for the same reasons we all hide or run away from things, fear. My son was hiding because he was scared and hiding made him feel safe. We all hide when things get hard. Lets face it, when storms come our way, we run to take cover, we find shelter to protect ourselves. Our first instinct is to go into isolation because it feels safe, we naturally push people away because we're scared.

The thing is isolation isn't safe at all. The enemy works best in isolation because he has you where he wants you and he will drown you with fear and suffocate you with anxiety. It's ok to take cover but you can't stay there for long. God is calling you to get up. We have to take a stand and rise up from all of this. It's time to leave that hiding place and show yourself. God allows you to hide but if you are going to do that, spend that time with God. He is always on the move and He's calling us to move too. Walking into our storms is scary but moving forward is the only way out, don't stay in it.

A lot of times we shrink ourselves according to our attack. We refer to ourselves as weak, but we forget God is strong and He will give us His strength, but we have to come out of hiding to use it. The day finally came and the long wait was over, it was finally time to go see the new doctor. The problem was, I couldn't find McGwire, he was hiding. He was hiding because he was scared. I found him where I expected he would be and bent down to his level and said, "Pal, we have to go. I know you're scared but this is the only way you're going to get better." I knew deep down he wanted to go, and get better but it was easier to hide and isolate himself because it felt safe to him. Going to a new unfamiliar doctor was scary and McGwire found more comfort in his hiding spot, so he hid.

McGwire had a meltdown. I tried to calm him down but it sent him into another panic attack and I had to get him through it. My husband had to come pick him up and carry him to the car. I hated to push him out of his comfort zone but he wasn't going to go on his own power. Sometimes it takes someone else to help you come out of hiding. We put him in the car and he fought us all the way there. He was scared to come out of hiding but that's what Satan does best is to convince you hiding is the only way, but that's far from the truth.

The only way is Jesus and He is calling you to rise up and go. Come out of your hiding spot. God is cheering for you and pushing you to go, but He can't do it for you. It's going to take you to get up and walk out of the shadows.

# CHAPTER 35

# Shadows

How do you survive each day when you're surrounded by darkness or when you wake up everyday in a dark place and go to bed every night with dark thoughts; when you feel consumed by the dark or the shade sets in and the shadows surround you and you're left in the dark? I felt so overwhelmed with darkness. I was sad and didn't know how to be happy anymore. I couldn't be happy, not until my son was better.

How do we find light again? First we have to step out from the shadows. What exactly is a shadow? Well by definition, a shadow is a dark area produced by a body coming between rays of light and a surface. In order for a shadow to be formed an object must block the light. At this time in my life, I was living in the shadows. Something was standing in my way blocking the light from coming in. Something kept me hidden and I desperately needed to find my way out.

In order to make a shadow you need an object to be translucent. If it's translucent it will let light partially pass through. What does it mean to have a translucent personality? It means you are free from a disguise or free from a coverup, what you see, is what you get. As people, we need to learn to be more translucent. We can't hide anymore, we have to come out from the shadows. We don't have to pretend we're ok when we're not.

When we are hurting, we have to talk to someone to help us. We have to quit covering up our pain and let it out of the shadows and bring it to the surface. We all want out of the dark, we strive for light, but why do we gravitate towards the shadows? I believe the shadows feel safe to us. We naturally try to find shade when things get too hot for us to handle. Shade is protection. We run to hide in the shade because we are afraid of getting burnt. We take ourselves into hiding because it feels safe to us but if you sit in the shade too long, you may adapt to the breeze and you won't be able to take the heat anymore. When my son was so sick, I spent a lot of time in the shade because I was scared to come out. I was stuck in a dark place for way too long but even when you're consumed by the dark and stuck in the shadows like I was, you need to know there's still light peaking through even though you can't see it.

Shadows can't be made unless you have light. God is the light, He is there in the shadows with you and has been there the whole time. This means that God has been with you through those long nights you cried and the lonely days you were in fog, He hasn't left your side while you have been consumed by the shadows. He provided shade for you. He casts a shadow for your safety but He doesn't want you to stay there forever, He wants you to come out of the shade and face the heat again. Come out of the shadows like I did. Absorb the rays of sunshine, because you will find happiness again. I eventually found my joy again but it took stepping out of the shadows and fighting back for the light that was blocked from me. Find peace in the shadows, find God.

# CHAPTER 36

# Speed Bumps

We finally reached the day I've been waiting for. It was time to take McGwire to the doctor. I was afraid to go and was scared of what they would say, but yet I knew we were headed to the right place. The ride to the doctors office was very unpleasant because McGwire was fidgeting in his seat the whole time and saying he didn't want to go. I promised him he could get a new beyblade if he was good.

During this time I offered little incentives to get him to go places. I hated to turn to that but it was the only leverage I had. McGwire wasn't as distant with me but yet he was still mean. I saw we had made some progress within the past month and I believe God had everything to do with that but our journey was far from being over. We had a lot of speed bumps on the road to his recovery. It wasn't going to be easy but hopefully the doctor would guide us in the right direction and we would finally get my son back. I had hope that day but I also was full of fear.

Recently I went to the lake to fish with my boys. As they fished, I typed trying to finish up my book. On the way we drove over some speed bumps and McGwire asked, "What's the purpose of speed bumps?" Patrick said, "To slow people down because you shouldn't be going fast or you could cause an accident." McGwire said, "Can you drive fast over them?" Patrick said, "Yes, but if you go too fast it can knock your wheels out of alignment." McGwire said, "Why do some people go fast over them then?" Patrick said, "Because some drivers aren't paying attention and they accidently hit them too fast or they're being impatient and reckless."

During this conversation I started thinking about this. God allows speed bumps in our lives. We went through a lot of speed bumps when McGwire was sick. There were times God had to slow us down because we were headed to disaster if we kept going at the pace we were. If you go too fast when God is telling you to slow down you will knock yourself out of alignment just like a car would. Once you knock yourself out of alignment, it's so hard to get on the straight path again. When we run like this for so long we become too tired and God needs us to be at rest so we can work for Him.

I've been running at full speed for a year hardly taking any time off. The speed bumps made me think about how busy life can get and how we start losing a grip on the things that are important to us. After going through all this with McGwire, God has been a big part of my life. I can't thank Him enough for what He has done for my family and therefore my desire these days is to be used by Him. I don't want to take a break because I want to do what His will has blessed me with. I have been walking down the path He created for me in my gym and I've been serving Him, but I need a day of rest. In order for me to help people, I need to take care of myself, my temple and because of this God has allowed some speed bumps in my life, seven days worth.

I'm using this time to spend with my family and work on this book so it will be ready for you. Don't ignore the speedbumps, slow down and stop when God calls you to stop and when He tells you to go, you need to go. At this point God was calling us to go to the new doctor, the one we weren't sure we could afford. He was a doctor that felt right, but was this the right path? We didn't know but we were moving by faith and on our way to find out. The advice given to us to get there? "Fill up on gas so you can continue on. G.A.S.= God and Spirit!"

# CHAPTER 37

# Fill Up On God's Spirit

Years ago my husband and I decided to go backroading. Before we had our kids we would do this often because it was a good way to slow down and spend some quality time together. We had some of our best and deepest conservations on those trips. We learned so much about each other on those backroad adventures. When we took off, we didn't pay attention to how much gas we had, we just went.

In Patrick's teenage years, he spent a lot of time riding on those old rugged roads, so he knew them well. When we went on those long drives, we used to play a game called try to get Patrick lost. Everytime we came across an intersection, Patrick would ask, right or left? I would pick the direction I thought looked unfamiliar and see if he knew his way. As we played the game, we talked about our busy lives and shared some laughs and we had a good time. I continued to pick the directions and before we knew it, we were lost. Patrick usually won but on this particular day, I won. I was happy I won, but the problem was we were getting low on gas and we were in the middle of nowhere.

Panic set in and we were running on fumes. As we continued making random rights and lefts, we found our game of trying to get Patrck lost suddenly turned into trying to get Patrick to find a familiar road. As we tried to conserve gas by coasting down the hills, in the distance we saw a little gas station and prayed we could make it there without running out of gas. As we paid for our gas, we realized we were in Cambridge, Ohio which was an hour away from home. We got off the backroads and found a familiar road and made our way back home.

My point of this story is you need to make sure you always fill up on gas before you take a long drive on some random backroad. This is also the same in life. Life is constantly having us take random rights and lefts and sometimes we get lost and end up on the wrong path that we never intended to go down. It took my son getting sick to help me find who God really was. I never knew God in the way that I discovered Him through this storm in my life. Through the battle of ups and downs with McGwire, I began my walk with God. I was new at it though and I wasn't sure how to carry on the relationship with Him.

Once you discover God, you don't want to let go of Him. His love has a magnetizing pull to it and the thought of losing that is scary. Life gets so busy and it's really easy to go down the wrong path. We sometimes forget about God and tend to drift from Him without even knowing it. With time, I discovered that an old gravel road was my connection to God. When I went for a run and listened to sermons and the Audio Bible, I realized it was how I developed on my relationship with God. I stayed connected to God by putting on my shoes and going for a run.

I started to see the transformation in myself as I was changing in small subtle ways. I was changing into a new person, a better person of what had always been; a person I never believed in until my son got sick. I looked at things in a new perspective. I was being filled with God's spirit as I ran. On the days I felt sad or stressed, I ran to paradise and reset myself. I felt a sense of peace when I was at the end of a run. I also realized on the days I felt sad it was Him that drew me to run. It didn't matter what state of mind I was in, when I ran, I felt full of God's spirit.

That's my point, we have to continuously stay close to God and fill up with His spirit just like we need to fill our cars up with gas. We are less likely to break down if we stay close to God. He is so much bigger than all of our problems but it doesn't feel that way when you drift from Him. We think our problems are bigger than God and we shrink according to the storm, but we are looking at it in the wrong perspective. When you stay close to God and know Him, when He speaks you'll be able to hear Him, not audibly, although some can, but in your heart. You will finally be able to see how much bigger He is than all your problems.

I didn't go to church for a really long time but I was invited to a church that I now attend regularly. When I leave church, I feel so uplifted and the presence of God strengthens me for that day. When Monday morning rolls around, I lose some of that strength and by the time I get to wednesday, I need another fill up because I am running low on God's spirit. By the time Sunday rolls back around, we have a whole new set of problems and have to start all over. Each week brings new trials.

This is the same with our vehicles. I used to drive almost two hours away for work. There is no way I could drive back and forth to work each day on one tank of gas. If I tried to do that, we know how that's going to turn out. I would find myself broken down on the side of the road in desperate need of help. You can't wait until you are completely empty to cry out for help or you will end up like your car, broken down.

Fill up with God continuously and you will find that your problems won't feel so big. Find your strength in God and get close to him and let him carry you through your week. We can't just rely on Sundays to carry us through. Especially when we know what Monday might bring. It's ok to keep making random right and left turns because that's life, but before you make those turns find the gas station in the distance and fill up your tank. Make sure God is the one telling you to make those turns and you will make it safely down the winding back road of life. Thank you Kathy Bebout for inviting me to church and helping me find my way to God. You have been a big part of my walk with God.

# CHAPTER 38

# The Breakthrough

I could see the doctor's office in the distance. The GPS said we would be there in one minute. When we finally arrived I was happy to be there but I was also nervous. My heart was pounding so hard, it felt like it was going to explode right out of my chest. I quickly whispered under my breath, we're here, we finally made it. A tear formed in my eye and I quickly wiped it away. I was ready for some answers. I sat there for a second and whispered a little prayer. "God, you guided us here, please let this doctor give us some answers."

McGwire said, "I don't want to go in there" I said "McGwire, I know you don't but you have to. You want that new beyblade don't you?" He said, "Yes." Just do this for us and we will get it after we see the doctor." He said "Fine, but this better be quick." As we walked through the front door, to the left of us was a separate set of doors and McGwire asked, "What's behind those doors?" I said "I don't know." Before I could stop him he swung the doors open and to our surprise there was a chapel. He wanted to know why there was a church in the doctor's office. When I saw the chapel, I knew that God was letting me know we were in the right place. I felt a sense of peace rush through me.

We opened the second set of doors and as we walked in we were greeted by the receptionist, she said hello, you must be McGwire. McGwire looked at her, then he looked at me puzzled and whispered, "How does she know my name?" She told McGwire to have a seat and that he would be taken back soon to see the doctor. There were lots of toys and he was told he could play with them if he wanted to. We looked around and there was a foosball table sitting in the middle of the waiting room with all kinds of other toys for kids to play with. McGwire ran over to me and said, "Mommy, my name is on that chalkboard!" He seemed so happy and I said, "Wow, that's cool pal."

It was so rare to see him smile. The chalkboard said welcome with McGwire's name on it with a list of other childrens names that were also being seen that day. I sat down next to him while he was playing with one of the toys and looked around the room and took it all in and felt a rush of peace flow through me. Finally a nurse came and called us back. She got McGwire's weight and height, then walked us to our room and did some other evaluations on him and said, "The nurse practitioner will be right back." McGwire asked "How long is this going to take?" I said, "Buddy, I don't know, I guess however long it needs to take. He said, "It better not take long or I'm leaving." McGwire was wearing a watch that day and said, "I'm timing this doctor to see how long it will take and if it takes any longer than thirty minutes I'm walking out of here." Patrick laughed and said, "Sure you are bud and how are you getting home?"

As we waited for the nurse practitioner to come in, McGwire found a cubby hole in the cabinets and went and sat in it. Patrick told him to get out of there before they came in. When the nurse practitioner walked into the room McGwire was still sitting in the cubby hole. She smiled and said, "You're fine buddy, you can stay there." She looked at me and Patrck and smiled and introduced herself, then said, "He likes to hide, huh?" I smiled back and introduced myself and said "Yes he does." She said, "That's good to know. hiding is a symptom of PANDAS." After asking a few questions, she had McGwire come out of the cubby hole so she could evaluate him. She did a number of tests on him.

She evaluated his coordination, balance and his fine motor skills. She listened to his belly and pushed on it and checked his joints and fingernails. She said, "He has a lot of zinc spots on his nails." I asked her, "What are zinc spots?" She said, "Do you see all these white spots on his fingernails?" She said those are called zinc spots and are an indication he is deficient in zinc. I found that very interesting. Then she proceeded to ask a series of questions. We had to answer them by choosing one of three options. Our choices were that he struggled with this always, sometimes or rarely. The list went on and on. I felt like I was taking a test. Every now and then McGwire would nudge me with his elbow tapping his watch. His watch at this point said we had been in there for 1 hr and 30 mins.

As time went on and we were still answering questions, McGwire proceeded to nudge me again showing me the time on his watch. He was mad and ready to go. This time we were looking at 2 hours and 30 mins. The nurse practitioner knew he was getting impatient and said, "I know buddy, this is taking a long time, we are almost done." I wasn't surprised but almost all my answers to her questions were always. I knew this was bad but yet these questions were designed because other kids struggled with the same things so this told me that we were in the right place and they understood what he has been going through.

She said, "I'm done with the questions but I need to step out for a minute and evaluate all this with the other doctor and we'll figure out a plan for him. The first thing I want to tell you is we'll be changing his antibiotic to a stronger one. The one he is currently taking isn't strong enough for this condition. I also saw he was on steroids and I'm glad he is no longer taking those. Steroids tend to make kids with PANDAS worse. In this office we like to get an extensive amount of blood work so we can see where McGwire is deficient and treat him there. We like to treat our kids from the inside out. We like to treat the gut first because the gut can be the root of a lot of the problems we see in these kids. We will be starting him on two types of probiotics so we can protect his gut while taking the long term antibiotic and if we can get his gut healthy a lot of times we see some symptoms diminish." I said, "Thank you so much, it feels good to finally have some answers." She smiled and said, "No problem at all." We will take good care of him," As she walked out of the room I felt blessed that my mom found this place. I knew this was where we needed to be.

As we waited for her to evaluate everything, McGwire became very antsy. He kept showing me the time on his watch, he was getting angry and ready to go. As we continued to wait in the room, to our surprise the doctor that I originally wanted to see popped his head in. He was the doctor on the video my mom showed me.

He said, "Hi, McGwire." He introduced himself to McGwire and shook his hand. He said, "Hey buddy, I've heard you're not feeling like yourself these days. You feel weird don't you? It was like everything changed all at once, huh." McGwire shook his head yes timidly. The doctor said, "It's not your fault bud. I have good news for you buddy, you're not alone in this. It isn't just you that suffers with this. Other kids have also been here to see us that feel just like you. You probably feel like nobody understands what you're going through but I do buddy. I know your head feels cluttered all the time. It's hard to do stuff without feeling overwhelmed. I also heard you don't like playing football or with your Legos anymore. I know you used to love that stuff but I have good news, you will love it again. You are at the right place buddy. We are going to help you feel better like you used to."

I watched McGwire while the doctor talked to him and I could tell he was getting through to him. McGwire was holding back tears because this doctor understood him, finally someone understood. The doctor looked over at me and Patrick and said, "Mom and dad, I want to let you know that you're going to get your son back. He will get better, we will make sure of that. I know this has been scary but you are in the right place now and we'll take care of him."

I teared up, to hear someone finally say those words. I said, "Thank you so much, you don't know how much that means to me to hear you say that." He smiled and said, "No problem at all." The doctor looked at McGwire and said, "McGwire you have a great mom and dad that love you very much and they did their homework and got you here just in time." The doctor looked over at Patrick and I and said "Mom and dad, I'm impressed you caught this when you did. Most of our kids that come in here are worse than McGwire, believe it or not. PANDAS can attack the spinal cord and that can cause them to not be able to walk or even more serious things. It is very rare that he hasn't reached that point yet. That was going to be the next step if you didn't get him in here when you did.

The doctor looked back at McGwire and said, "Look at it like this McGwire, it's like your brain has been hijacked, like someone stole what was yours but we are going to get back what was taken from you. I know your scared buddy but it's all uphill from here." I teared up, it felt so good to hear him say that. I said, "Thank you so much, you have been a blessing to our family. Finding you has been a true miracle." He smiled and said, "I've been where you are, I know how you feel. I have a son that is autistic, so I get it. My goal has always been to help other kids like him. You're here now and he is in good hands, I promise."

The doctor left and the nurse practitioner came back in. She said to McGwire, "I heard the doctor came in and talked to you McGwire." She sat down beside me and handed me a list of supplements she wanted us to start with. She said it was up to us if we bought the supplements because the insurance didn't cover them. I was scared to purchase everything because we had to pay for the appointment out of pocket and now we had these supplements but I didn't care. I was going to buy everything that he needed to get better. I trusted them and I trusted God.

As we checked out, the receptionist said, "We need you to go get his blood work done." She gave us directions on how to get there. As we walked out of the office, I saw the chapel we passed on the way in. I said, "I want to stop here." McGwire asked, "Why do you want to go to church?" I smiled and said, "I just want to see it." We walked in. I sat down on one of the pews and shed a few tears. I said softly, "Thank you God, thank you for guiding us here." Our prayers were finally being answered. I gave God the glory and praise for that.

It has been a long road for us, but we finally had some answers. We finally found people that understood. It felt good to hand this over to the doctor and let him take control so the weight didn't have to fall on our shoulders anymore. It's the little things in life we take for granted. We need to feel fortunate that on these days our kids are healthy, because when they're not and they suddenly become sick, you lose your grip on everything. Everything falls apart and you become broken.

If I could have changed everything, I would have. If I could have savored those hugs a little more and taken more time to have enjoyed those moments my family laughed together, I would have. If I could have taken the place of Mcgwrie being sick, I would have stepped in and taken this from him. The fact is, I couldn't change any of it. There will always be regrets and you will always blame yourself through difficult moments but don't. I would change everything in a heartbeat but I can't.

We have to learn to embrace that God sent a storm for a reason and we have to learn to trust the process and lean into God a little more. I had learned to rely on God in the midst of McGwire's illness. It didn't come easy at first and at times I still struggle with it. These are the things that helped me understand that worrying didn't help to bring McGwire's healing. It made things worse.

I understand now that God is the ultimate healer of all things. I left that office feeling God's presence upon me. I felt His inner peace. We had to go get McGwire's blood work and by God's grace we didn't have to fight him to do it, he was a brave little boy that day. As we rode back home McGwire fell asleep in the backseat with his new beyblade in his hand, I knew God was riding in the car with us that day. We were on our way to our blessing, this was our breakthrough, but it wasn't going to be easy. We had a lot of work to do, but we were on our way to victory. It was going to be a long road. We knew we had a few more speed bumps coming our way but we were getting there by the grace of God.

# CHAPTER 39

# Treadmill Rage

We will go through seasons in life, good seasons and bad. The break between day and night will help us see the signs of the season we are in. Day and night is the separation of a new day and a new day can be the difference between a battle and a breakthrough. We all know when we have been in the long season of winter and spring is about to come. We start to hear the birds chirping, the leaves on the trees start to come back nice and green and it doesn't look as dark and gloomy outside anymore. The sun starts peeking in from time to time and it starts to warm up.

We know that in the season of spring, we will have good days and bad days. We might wake up to a rainy day but we may also wake up and see little glimpses of the sun too. Each night will bring forth a new day. This is the same in our lives. You may be in a dark season in your life right now but as you walk through this season, spring will eventually arrive and the sun will rise. When McGwire was sick, we were stuck in the long season of winter. It never felt like there was a finish line to what we were going through. It never felt like spring was ever going to come. Everyday it was dark, cold and dreary. When McGwire started taking his new antibiotic and supplements, I started to see some changes in him that were good. I was starting to see little glimpses of my son again. This gave me hope that we were on our way to a breakthrough.

Giving McGwire the supplements wasn't an easy process though. This was all new to me. When I first started giving the supplements to him, I was overwhelmed. I had to give him one supplement at a time to make sure he didn't react badly to it. As I added another supplement every other day, I would evaluate him and see if he was responding to it ok. The problem with these supplements is that he had so many to take and it was a fight to get him to take them. He didn't know how to swallow tablets so I had to mix them into chocolate milkshakes. To this day, McGwire hates chocolate milkshakes.

As time went by he was taking all of his supplements and I was starting to see a lot of improvement in him but he wasn't by any means cured. He had a lot of flares. Flares are like a relapse. The relapses would occur when he was exposed to another virus or to an allergen or even stress. Sometimes when he would flare, his symptoms would increase and last longer with every episode. This caused a lot of anxiety in me because I saw him backsliding a lot and I was at a point that I had high hopes we were into the next season. We may not have been in the season of spring yet but we were in the transition between winter and spring. This was progress but my mind sometimes focused on the bad and forgot all about the good.

I want to remind you what spring is. Spring is full of hope, it's a reminder that God is all about making things new. God created day and night so we could see the change and to know that maybe today was hard but tomorrow will be better. Winter is such a long season but so is the battle you are up against. Spring is a reminder of new life. Maybe you feel like things are not changing for you. Maybe you feel broken and lost. Maybe you feel lifeless and you are just going through the motions. Maybe you had big dreams but currently they have been crushed and they feel dead to you.

I want to remind you that tomorrow is a new day and spring is on its way and it's the season of change. Spring is the season of life after death. When Easter finally arrives we know we are closer to those nice sunny days. Easter reminds us that Jesus rose from the grave and He is alive. I know life doesn't feel good right now but the change of the season is coming and you will rise from it too.

My son was sick and that was the reality I woke up to everyday. When I saw glimpses of my son again, it gave me hope. One day when you wake up it won't be dark anymore because spring will settle in and the sun will rise! My son was rising up from his sickness just like the son, Jesus, rose from His grave. The grave couldn't hold the power of Jesus and it won't hold you either. So look for the light, it's found in the Son.

Don't let Satan convince you that things aren't going to change, just start focusing on the good and not so much on the bad. McGwire was making progress but Satan changed my way of thinking and this is how I handled it.

McGwire was getting better, but we had a long road ahead of us. I knew we were not there yet, but when I looked deep into his eyes, I knew he was in there. I just needed to find him. We were starting to have good days with McGwire and on those days I became stronger and I fought harder. On the bad days, when he flared, I wanted to give up. I felt like I was starting all over again. I wanted all good days and that just wasn't happening yet. I was being impatient. I was constantly on the edge of my seat with my fists up ready for the battle. The problem that comes from the good days and bad days is when bad things have happened in your life, you get to the point you're afraid of it happening again. We put our guard up and we're waiting for the next disaster. We have to cast out the wrong way of thinking and choose to think right. We need to find a safe place to occupy our minds so we learn how to release our emotions.

For me I take it out in the gym or on a run. So you may have to take a walk, or call a good friend, and find something to take the weight off your chest. Put your energy into something else instead of putting your energy into the storm you are up against. Don't let Satan steal what Jesus died on the cross to give you. Isolating yourself is not the answer, the answer is to move forward even when you don't want to. What we don't feel like doing sometimes is actually what we need to do.

That all being said, I want to paint a picture for you and explain to you how I handled some deep emotions I never dealt with. The problem with that is they will eventually catch up to you and will overflow into an emotional breakdown. This isn't a proud moment of mine, and maybe I didn't handle it well, but that is what happens when you harbor emotions. There is a lesson learned here. That's why I am writing this book for you, so you learn how to handle your emotions in the right way and not let them get the best of you. I was so mentally exhausted, I was at my breaking point and I had enough. I had a sick child and I just wanted him to be better. McGwire was having a lot of good days but this day in particular McGwire was having a flare. It was one of those difficult days and my guard was up. I couldn't handle another bad day. I wanted it to be over, I didn't want to be on this emotional rollercoaster anymore, I was done.

When my husband got home from work he sensed something was wrong. It was written all over my face. The tension was there. Patrick said to me, "How was your day?" He already knew the answer by the way I was pacing around the house picking things up. He knew I was in a bad place. I said, "Not good." He walked over and wrapped his arms around me and stopped me in my tracks. He kissed my cheek and whispered in my ear, "You need some time to yourself. Why don't you go work off some stress in the basement."

Our gym was in our basement and he knew I needed to step away for a little bit. I looked at him and said, "No." I never wanted to leave my kids and do something for me. I didn't want to put all this on Patrick. I felt guilty. I looked at Patrick with tears in my eyes, and said, "I just want all this to just go away. I want McGwire to be better." Patrick hugged me and said, "He is getting better Cass. Today was just a bad day but the bad days are getting less and less. It's going to be a process that we have to walk through." I shook my head and said, "You're right." He turned me around to face him and looked me in the eyes and said, "Cass, just go workout, let off some steam, it will make you feel better. We will be fine. I got the boys."

It was raining that day so I couldn't go for a run. The next best thing was to get on the treadmill. I grabbed my shoes and went down to my gym. I didn't really feel like working out that day, I was too drained but I needed a release. I hopped onto the treadmill and started walking. I felt out of breath at the beginning . When I started feeling a little warmed up, I started to jog at 5mph. My mind was so overwhelmed and filled with negativity. I didn't know what to do to help McGwire. I felt helpless. McGwire was starting to show improvement but now we were back to square one. I guess I didn't understand the concept of PANDAS. I was seeing little glimpses of my boy again. I needed him to keep moving forward but he kept backsliding. I needed to meditate on those positive thoughts but my mind automatically went to the negative thoughts.

I bumped the treadmill up to 6 mph. I continued thinking about everything. I thought we were on track with everything, but when he had bad days like this, I felt like we were starting all over. These backslides drove me crazy. I wanted to keep moving forward. This stop and go stuff wasn't working for me. I felt sad but my sadness quickly turned to bitterness. I was mad. Mad at myself for not being able to understand or comprehend all this. I was mad at God for letting this battle go on for so long.

I increased my speed to 7 mph. I was so angry, I began thinking about a year ago and how our family was happy and complete, but look at us now. We are in a never ending battle. I couldn't see the victory in this. We were not prepared for all this and it felt like it wasn't going away anytime soon. My mind began thinking this is the way it's going to be forever. This is our life now. We have a sick child. Will we ever overcome this? I was sad but I was angry.

I aggressively pushed 8 mph on the treadmill. Sweat was running down my face. I started to get out of breath, but I didn't care. This pain felt better than the raw pain I felt inside. I thought about stopping the treadmill because I was getting tired. I didn't feel like I had the energy in me to run like this but I kept going anyway. I thought to myself, you have been out of breath for a long time, what's the point of stopping now. I dug deeper into my dark thoughts. I was developing a rage inside of me as I ran vigorously on the treadmill. I wanted God to take this away right now. I wanted Him to fix my son on my terms, on my time. I put a deadline on God as if He worked for me, as if I was the one in control, not Him. I was trying to take control of this battle. I knew I handed my children over to God but I wanted them back. I knew God was supposed to help me fight but I didn't like it being out of my control. It made me feel too vulnerable and too weak. My son needed a win. My family needed a win.

I thought I can't control this mess my family's in. I can't control my son's pain but I can control this treadmill so I aggressively pushed 9 mph and began sprinting. The treadmill was my warzone and it might have been a machine but it was my weapon. I was fighting this battle by the power of the buttons. My breathing was rapid, my legs were tired but I kept going.

I began thinking about McGwire and the way he used to hug

me and love me and how he was my sweet little boy. Then I began thinking about his pale face and the dark circles around his eyes. He was lost and confused and so was I. I wanted to be the hand he held, the hand that would pull him out of this pit he fell into but I couldn't. I knew it had to be God's hands to pull him out. I was his mother. I was supposed to be able to fix his pain and be his comfort. I began fading as I ran and drifted into a deep thought. My legs were moving so fast but it was as if time slowed down and God hit pause and I began thinking about the first night I saw a little glimpse of my son coming back to me.

One night McGwire was having one of his flares and I couldn't get him to do his homework. He threw himself on the floor and cried like a toddler, kicking and screaming. I bent down to his level and looked into his eyes and said, "McGwire get up, you can do this homework. You know this stuff. You're smart. You need to fight this and just get up and do it. You need to reset yourself." As I looked at his black swollen pupils, I knew his brain was inflamed and causing this. I said, "You need to get in the shower and refocus and we'll tackle the homework when you get out."

Getting McGwire in the shower was always a struggle but for some reason that night, he did it without a fight. When he got out of the shower, he walked into the kitchen and looked me in the eyes. For the first time I saw a little sparkle of blue in his eyes. I looked deep into his eyes and teared up because I hadn't seen his crystal blue eyes for a long time. He sat down at the kitchen table and worked on his homework with no fight. He didn't say anything. He just sat down and did his homework. I couldn't believe it.

That night as I layed in bed with him and told him his bedtime story, he stopped me and said, "Mommy." and I said, "Yes bud." He said, "I'm sorry." I was completely caught off guard and we both began to cry. But those two little words were magic to my ears. He was never sorry, he constantly told me everything was all my fault. He said, I'm so sorry for tonight and for everything I've done. I can't help it. I don't want to be bad. I try so hard to be good but I can't control it. I'm trying to fight it but I can't. I hesitated to grab his hand because I didn't want to ruin the moment but I reached in and took it softly anyway. He usually would pull away but not this time. He let me take hold of it and I squeezed it tight. I wanted to savor this moment.

I composed myself enough to say, "It's okay McGwire. This is not your fault. This is not you pal. You're just sick but you are getting better. I can see you fighting it right now. Keep fighting, and know you don't have to fight alone. Mommy is here to fight with you. We are going to win this battle pal, I promise. We can do it." He reached over and hugged me. Tears flooded from my eyes. That was the first hug I had from him since he got sick. I had to compose myself from crying too hard and I needed to stay strong for him. I hugged him tight and rubbed his back. I didn't want to let go. When he finally fell asleep, I turned to my back and layed there looking up at the ceiling and began crying. I said, "Thank you God. Thank you so much." That night I realized the battle wasn't over. We had a chance. I finally had some hope. I was going to keep fighting for him. I realized that night, he was starting to fight too.

I faded back to reality and found myself in tunnel vision sprinting on the treadmill. I was sweating profusely. My legs were weak and I barely could breathe. My heart was about to pound out of my chest. I wanted to stop the treadmill and be done but I couldn't. I started thinking, I can't stop now, McGwire didn't have a stop button with his sickness like I did on the treadmill. He had to endure all his pain and torment so I decided I was going to endure it too. The way I felt on the treadmill was the way McGwire felt everyday.

The only way I was going to relate to him and understand what he was going through was to keep running on the treadmill. I had to run this race like he was. I had to feel what he was feeling. I needed to suffer like he was suffering, I would never relate to him if I didn't have something to relate to. Everything was out of my control with this battle we were in; the only thing I could control was the treadmill so I pressed 10mph and ran faster. My legs could barely keep up but I kept going. I told myself to fight like your son is. I wanted to hurt like he was. I saw what all this did to him from the outside but I needed to know what it felt like on the inside. I wanted to take the pain from him here on the treadmill. I wanted to fight for him through this run.

I was mixed with emotions. I was angry, sad and vulnerable all at the same time. I was determined I wasn't going to break. I wasn't going to quit, that wasn't an option. I had to keep going even if it hurt. I had to keep pressing through for McGwire. I was struggling to keep up, but life felt like more of a struggle than the treadmill did. I needed this run like McGwire needed to fight. Things were getting dark and I could barely breathe. I knew I was pushing my limits. I knew this wasn't healthy. I was going too far but I didn't want to quit. If I endure this fight on the treadmill then I could become stronger for McGwire. How far was I going to take this? How far was too far? I began to fade in and out and suddenly something came upon me, a voice, saying STOP. I pressed stop and I collapsed to my knees on the treadmill.

I was shaking. I felt weak and tired. I was gasping for air. Tears poured from my eyes. I thought to myself, this must be how McGwire felt. When McGwire drops to his knees in a tantrum, it's because he feels like this. I understood what he was feeling now. I was still angry. I was angry my son had to feel like this, I wanted it to be me to feel like this. I wanted to take it from him so I did it down here in this gym. I found strength back in my legs and I got off the treadmill and walked over to an old tractor tire propped against the wall and I aggressively shoved it over and grabbed my husband's old baseball bat and started swinging it as hard as I could at the tractor tire. I began to cry as I hit the tire. The harder I hit it, the harder I cried.

Then I started to swing the bat faster and faster and suddenly I heard a voice inside my head say ENOUGH, YOU'RE DONE. I dropped to my knees and began sobbing, laying my head against the tractor tire. I let it all out, everything that was built up inside of me, I released it all. I laid back and spread my sweat covered body on the cool concrete floor and stared up at the ceiling. I put all my pain to rest in this workout, I had nothing left. I prayed to God and said, "I'm sorry God, I need you to take control, not me." I suddenly developed a sense of peace inside my soul and I slowly got up off the floor.

I took a few deep breaths and began to stand up with shaky legs. I felt a sense of relief. It felt good getting these trapped emotions out of me and putting the fight back in. I felt weak from the workout but yet I felt stronger at the same time. I needed to start over and go see my family. I felt like I could approach McGwire again with clarity and understanding. I knew the pain he was enduring, I understood what he has been feeling now. I went through this storm with him in my own way. I was reset and ready to tackle anything that came my way. I had faith and I had hope.

God visited me in my gym that day. He allowed me to take control of the treadmill but He taught me that this is what happens when I try to control things. I ended up flat on my back crying for help. God may have let me control the treadmill but when I control things, I don't get anywhere, not without Him. God let me push the buttons this time but He stopped me before I went too far. God was teaching me a lesson and that was never take the lead because His way is the best way. God allowed me to do this because I finally understood why McGwire has been struggling. I got to feel what he has been feeling this whole time. McGwire has been feeling like he has been stuck on a treadmill running and getting nowhere but today God finally pushed stop on McGwire's battle.

I walked upstairs ready to see my family. I opened the door to find them peacefully sitting in the living room playing a Pokemon game on the nintendo switch. McGwire came running over to me and said, "Come see what Pokemon I caught." Larkin came running over excited too. I bent down and hugged both of my boys and they hugged me back. I was so excited to sit down on the couch with my boys and watch them play their game.

McGwire was back to himself. The boy I have missed for so long. He was back and he was happy. I couldn't help but just stare at his precious face as he played his game because he was finally smiling. A smile that was true and sincere. God allowed me to have a moment that day. It may be a moment I wasn't proud of but it was a moment I needed. I may have had a breakdown but it was my own version of restoration.

God was using that moment to teach me that my gym was an outlet. It was an outlet for me that day, but now it's an outlet for others. My gym may not be a church and I may not see a prophet, but it's my ministry. Today I use the gym to help people overcome their anxieties by sweating them out and fighting back with a bat and a tire. They can lay all their fears to rest in the gym like I did. When someone is at the end of themselves and having a bad day, I hand over the ball bat and let them unleash their pain on the old tractor tire. I told you this story because I think you needed the illustration of what can happen when you're having mixed emotions.

I'm definitely not telling you to be hard on your body, and do what I did. You should take care of your body, it's your temple that God gave you. I shouldn't have done what I did but that's where I was mentally and sometimes when you are mentally exhausted like I was, we make poor decisions.

Telling you this story was hard but I know you needed to hear it because maybe this is where you are mentally too. I want to tell you that I understand what you are going through. We all get to a point that we break, but that break is where God puts us back together. That break is a breakdown but that is where we find the strength to get back up. God didn't allow me to break all the way, he just allowed me to take it to the point that all I had left was Him. I learned that day that your battle doesn't define your outcome. The Devil doesn't have the last say, God does.

You have to trust the process that God is leading you through. Even if you don't see the light yet, you have to keep looking for it because the light is there and it's about ready to shine in, so open up your eyes and look for the sun. This is the season of change and spring is coming. Go run for it. Watch for the Son to rise, because the day will come and there will be joy in the morning.

# CHAPTER 40

# Trails

I have been running back roads for a while now. I try to go to my favorite backroad Paradise as often as I can. Recently my husband made some trails in our woods. My workout class needed a challenge so I have been having them strap on rucksacks and hit the trails.

A lot of times when I run, I take my dog Jazz. She isn't a Ranger by any means, but she's my new best friend and is a great running partner. She loves to run! She knows when I am about to take off for a run. She knows all the steps I go through to get ready. If she sees me grab my ear buds and put on my shoes, she knows it's time to run. She can't control her excitement. She knows she's going with me once I grab her running harness and leash.

Today I didn't have a lot of time for a run so I decided I would run the trails my husband made. Since we were at my house, I had the bright idea that I didn't need a leash for Jazz. I figured she would run by my side so I wouldn't have to mess with hooking her up. I got my shoes on and placed my earbuds in and took off, I said, "Come on Jazz" and she was puzzled. She just stood there. She knew I missed a step and she needed her harness put on. I said, "Let's go Jazz, it's ok, you don't need your harness today." I took off again and she followed me this time. The trails were new to both of us.

The way my husband made them, there were lots of twists and turns, so I winged it and just ran. Jazz ran ahead of me and she kept looking back at me not sure which way she needed to turn. I was constantly directing her which way to go. This continued to go on and before long Jazz started to take her own path. She started to get off the trail and started running around in the woods. I was getting irritated because I was scared she was going to take off to the neighbors house. When I wasn't looking, she would drift away.

As we continued the run, I kept trying to enjoy the run but Jazz wasn't allowing me too because she kept taking off. I would have to stop and yell for her and she would come running back. Before long I decided this wasn't working and went and got her leash and harness. When I hooked her up, we ran again and she did so much better as she ran by my side and she knew she couldn't lead because she didn't know the path. This trail was new to her and she needed me to guide her.

God revealed something to me that I think is important enough to share with you. God placed me on a new path when McGwire got sick. This path was very unfamiliar to me and it had a lot of twists and turns on it too. I found myself being like Jazz, without a leash. I kept trying to lead myself down this trail. I took the wrong turns and I felt myself getting lost and not realizing that I drifted away from God.

I realized something today, Jazz can't run without her leash. We tried it and it didn't work, it will never work for her. I could try it over and over and she will always drift away from me. Jazz loved the freedom of running at her own pace and stopping when she wanted to stop and going when she wanted to go. What jazz didn't know is if she drifted too far from me she could get lost or even worse, she could get hit by a car or attacked by another animal.

It's the same with us. We need to remain close to God and let Him lead us. We like the freedom to make our own choices and go at our own pace. We like to quit when we feel like quitting, we like to run ourselves so busy until we can't go anymore. But when we lead we may drift too far and we won't even know we are doing it. We will get lost, like Jazz or we'll get hit by something we didn't see coming. If we choose the wrong path, Satan will come in for the attack.

The good news is God can guide you back in the right direction, but you have to be like Jazz and listen for His voice like she listens for mine. God is calling you back to the path. Jazz has to have a leash, we do too. The leash keeps us close to God. So the question is what is your leash? How do you remain close to God? If someone told me in order to remain close to God you have to sit down and read the Bible,

I would have never done it. Why?

Back then, It wouldn't have been that easy. We all have different forms of worship, mine is done in movement. I am not a person that can just sit and read. My mind drifts too much and I get distracted way too easily. Movement allows my mind to settle and calm down. God used my mom to send me sermons on my phone because she knew my form of worship would be done in movement. I'm not good at sitting and reading the Bible but I can listen to it. God knew He could train me and do work in me through the form of running.

My suggestion is find your hobby, we all have one but we have to find it and when we do, we need to invite God into it. Running is my passion and it's my hobby. It was my hobby before I found God. Running became my outlet during the time McGwire was sick. Eventually everything in this world at some point of our lives will fade out and we drift from it because of our busy lives. Once you invite God into your life, it will never fade away unless you start running without your leash. Our passion for our hobbies will remain if God is a part of it.

I stick to running because God is with me through it. There are a lot of times I don't feel like running but I do it anyway because it's how I stay connected to God, it's my leash. Find your outlet and connect it with God. Maybe it's not running, maybe it's art, or music, or hunting, whatever it may be, invite God into it and it will become even more important to you. It will become your purpose in life. The only way I was able to write this book for you was because of my desire to run. I have learned so much about God on these runs. That's how He works.

When I first started running and listening to these sermons, God used these runs as my outlet to help me with my struggles and now these runs have become my classroom so I can write to you to help you through your struggles too. Maybe you are lost but you don't have anyone guiding you the right way. Maybe you don't know where to turn so you continue to sink deeper into your struggles. I want to help you find your way, that is why I wrote this book, I wrote it for you. I want to be that hand that pulls you out of your pit. I want to be that voice that tells you it's going to be ok. I want to be that person that pushes you to get up and rise out of this. I didn't write this book just to tell you my family's testimony, I wrote this book to help you make yours.

God is working on you right now. It may be a test but one day it will be your testimony and you will be able to talk about it just like I am right now. You will be able to use that testimony to help others. I was fortunate through my storm because I had a husband that believed in me and kept me from giving up on things. I wanted to give up all the time but he was constantly dragging me out of bed and making me face my day. There were days I didn't want to move but he made me move anyway.

I had a mom that never stopped sending me sermons, she kept pushing me towards God but not in an overwhelming way. I had a baby to take care of and a sick child to get better. I couldn't give up, those were my reasons to keep fighting and to keep pressing through even when it hurt. My boys were my "why." You have a "why" too. You have a reason why to keep going, a reason why to keep fighting. You have to fight through this.

That's why this book has found its way into your hands because God is calling you and it's time to surrender and let Him take the lead. This is your leash. Find your outlet and get reconnected to God. The blessing isn't found in the woods, the breakthrough is found on the trail, maybe the trail is new, but stick to it and follow God and you will find your breakthrough on this new path He is leading you on.

# CHAPTER 41

# Homework

McGwire had good days and bad days. Homework was a real struggle for him. Kids with PANDAS struggle with tasks. They can't process things very well because their minds are too cluttered. We have to remember their minds, as our doctor put it, are hijacked

With PANDAS, there is a lot going on inside their brains that people on the outside can't see. We can't see the scary intrusive thoughts, self doubts and horrific visions that are going on inside their heads. They are full of worries and fears and we can't see how crowded their minds are. We are clueless on how heavy their brain fog is because we haven't gone a mile in their shoes nor would we want to.

I had to learn to be compassionate during this time because his behavior was due to the hidden symptoms that I didn't understand or relate to. The teachers in his life had to learn to process this and work around it. We dealt a lot with meltdowns with McGwire when it came to tasks, especially homework.

It got to the point we didn't know what was going to happen with him academically. I was so scared he would fall behind. I didn't want all this for him. I wanted him to thrive but how could he in this condition? I took the information to our principal at McGwire's school and he was completely supportive. He said he would help us through this.

I also took the information to McGwire's teacher and she was very sympathetic through this time. She noticed a change in McGwire too. She allowed me to message her every morning to update her on what condition McGwire was in so she could be prepared for what to expect out of him. She was so good and would evaluate him daily and let me know how he was doing in school. Sometimes I got good reports and sometimes she would tell me he was very robotic. A lot of times he would just stare off in space and it was like no one was home. You couldn't get anything out of him.

I finally decided to tell her the struggles we were having with him doing his homework. One day she took it upon herself to help him do his homework before they left school. She continued to do this everyday. We no longer had to struggle with McGwire doing his homework. She took away hours of pain, crying and fighting that we used to have to go through every night. She allowed us to have our evening back. We had one less thing to worry about, because of that one simple task she did for us.

The thing is, she didn't have to do that but she did it anyway. God placed her on our path through this hard time in our lives and I was so thankful for that. She made it so much easier for us. We went through panic attack after panic attack and tantrum after tantrum. Some of our worst evenings we had with McGwire was wrapped around homework. She didn't realize how much she did for us.

Some of the most simple things in life might make some of the biggest impacts in someone else's life. We have to do the small stuff for people even if we feel like it won't make a difference, because the small stuff might be exactly what the other person needs. I will always remember this very special teacher for the rest of my life.

It's so funny how life circles around because the same teacher is now part of my workout family and I'm so blessed to have her in my life. I told her how thankful I was to have her as McGwire's teacher at the hardest time in our lives. I told her she helped us so much by helping him with his homework. She said it was no problem at all. Our evenings were better because we didn't have that battle we had to fight anymore. I was able to play beyblades with McGwire and battle him that way instead of battling him to do homework.

Misti Clemens, I want to thank you so much for everything you did for my family. You were there for McGwire, and never gave up on him and you helped us through one of the biggest battles we had during this time. You will never know how much this meant to us. You are and always will be our favorite teacher of all time! You were placed on our path for a reason and you are back on my path again and I'm so thankful you are a part of our lives again!

# CHAPTER 42

# Rucksack

While writing this book, my family and I have experienced enough challenges to write a book of its own. As we experienced one traumatic thing after another, I often closed my laptop and stopped typing. I didn't feel like I could walk you through your traumatic experience while I was living out my own.

Today I decided to open my laptop and start again. Lately my body has become drained and tired. I'm halfway through this book and I find myself at a loss for words. I know the story isn't over yet. I know for your healing and mine, the story must go on but today I'm tired. I keep running into roadblocks. The season is changing now and so am I. Today my body feels like it's failing. I'm exhausted.

I've been so busy, and I'm grateful for that, but I'm feeling so run down, and so sluggish. I'm tired because of the race of life but sometimes we're tired because we're up against so much pain that's dragging us down. Are you tired too? Are you fighting something that is draining you? Did you build a wall to protect yourself through this battle but now you find yourself trying to break through that wall but it won't move? Are you working around something that God intends you walk through?Sometimes we use a lot of energy trying to walk around the path that God wants us to go on. Don't avoid it, walk into it.

The point is, I'm tired right now and so are you and those are the facts. We are tired and we are tired of being tired. So what do we do about it? We have to get up and face it. We have to keep trying and if we get knocked down, we get up and we try again. We fight back and use the energy we have, even if it's not a lot. You might be tired but you're breathing and if you're breathing, you're living and if you're living that means God is going to use you. You are important!

Lets face it, the Devil wouldn't be placing this on you if he was threatened by you and God wouldn't be allowing this to happen if He wasn't intending to use it for your good. I have been fighting so hard trying to write this chapter, I've been at a loss for words and I want to say this in the right way for you to understand. I want my words to sink deep down into your heart so it gives you the energy to get back up again. I want to set a fire inside of your soul to make you feel alive again and to remind you that you are still breathing. You are alive and you still have the fight left in you.You still have something so powerful inside you but you have to resurface it. I have so much to say to you but where do I start. Everytime I open my laptop, I get stuck. I find myself staring at a blank screen.

Today, I decided to pick up my computer and just type what's on my mind. This is all raw material. My words are coming from deep down inside my heart. Don't give up, you are so close to breakthrough, so don't stop now, keep going. You're almost there. I am telling you this because I've been where you are, I've sat where you've sat, I've cried like you've been crying. I needed someone to help me get up again and help pull me out of the rut I was in. It took the right words for me to hear to get me to stand up again and I want to do that for you. I didn't go through this storm to just sit here and keep my testimony to myself. I'm here to bring you back on your feet too. I was bound to the chains of my son's sickness.

Those chains limit you so you have to stand up and God will release them from you. It might not happen overnight but within time you will see that those chains were not designed to be stuck in, they were designed to help others. The seasons may change and you are going to experience change in your life but God never changes.

My journey on this backroad blessing has been a rough one, with lots of hills and terrain. I've run into a pothole from time to time but one thing I have learned is nothing can stop you with God by your side. I've been feeling cold and numb lately and I don't know why. I thought about laying down and resting. I tried but I couldn't. I'm feeling too irritable and restless. I found myself driving over to my favorite backroad, Paradise. I knew I needed to be there, not on the couch.

Before I left the house, I decided to grab my 20 pound rucksack. Honestly, I don't know what compelled me to grab it but I did. Running with tired legs and heavy shoulders wasn't ideal for the way I was already feeling. When I arrived, I felt confined to my car, not wanting to run but I made myself get out and go. I strapped my rucksack onto my back. It felt heavy. As I began running, I knew this wasn't going to be easy. I began to think to myself, why am I doing this? Why am I running with added weight when I already felt weighed down as it was? Am I being reckless to my already worn out body? Maybe, but I kept going anyway.

My breathing was off right from the beginning. My legs felt like they could give out any second and the rucksack felt heavier than I could ever remember. As my thoughts took over as I ran, I began to see what God was teaching me for the purpose of this book. Five years ago my world came crashing down on me. My son was sick. It was five years ago that I began to run on this road.

When I started running here, I was lost and scared, but running on this road was my outlet. It started as a run but as time went by, it became my time with God. On these runs I finally began to listen to the sermons my mom was constantly sending me. I started to absorb every word that was being said. I learned who Jesus was. I didn't know Jesus, not like that. I didn't have Him as a friend. It wasn't until one day, I turned my sermon off and I prayed as I ran down this old rugged road. That's when it began.

Back then, was I running away from my faith or was I running to find it? Was I running away from God or was I running towards Him? To be honest, I had no idea what I was doing. I was just putting on my shoes and going for a run. I thought I was going for a run but little did I know, I was moving towards something. That's the point I'm trying to make, sometimes you don't know what you are doing, you're just going with it. You won't always have the answers to why you are moving or you may not know where you're headed but you just have to go. I was going, I was running.

I had an appointment with Jesus back then and I didn't even

know it. I didn't know when I was running, I was running to God but it's because He was chasing after me. You can run away from God but He will never stop chasing you because He loves you. This road was where I first found Jesus. I found myself back here today, but this time I had a rucksack on my back. Why? Because I had another appointment with Jesus, but this time He was teaching me something very important. He was teaching me something to share with you.

God was calling me back. He said, "Go back to the first place you found me." Don't just lay here and dwell on all the reasons why you shouldn't go. You will always find a million reasons to talk yourself out of something. You just have to go. Five years ago I felt like I was carrying the weight of the world on my shoulders and today God wanted to remind me what that felt like. He wanted me to remember so I could write this for you. God knows what's in you. He knows your gifts and weaknesses. He knows your trauma and your testimony. He knows your pain and your scars.

When I strapped on the 20 lb rucksack today, I remembered how it felt to struggle. I remembered how it felt to be completely out of breath. How hard it was to just move. How hard it was to take a few steps forward. The rucksack reminded me of five years ago when I carried all my burdens on my shoulders by not letting go and handing it over to God. The rucksack reminded me that I can take it off. I don't have to wear it. I can unbuckle the strap and remove the rucksack off of my shoulders.

Sometimes going through a storm can be heavy on the shoulders. When you are up against something, you have to move through it even if it's hard to move. We can't stop just because we are tired, we have to keep going. I ran two miles with the rucksack on. I wanted to take it off right when I started, but I knew I would sabotage what God was trying to show me so I kept going.

When I saw my car in the distance, I knew I was close to my destination and when I got there I would be able to take the rucksack off. I kept my eyes on my car because I knew if I focused on that, I would keep going because I was almost there. You have to keep your eyes on Jesus, because you are so close to making that breakthrough. When you reach your destination God is leading you to, you will be able to unload that rucksack off your shoulders. God will take the weight you've been carrying and He will carry it for you. Hand everything over to Jesus because He never intended you to carry it.

When I reached my car, I took off the rucksack and I knew God wasn't done with me yet. He wanted me to run another two miles without it. He needed me to see how much better I felt with the weight off my shoulders. He was showing me that carrying the weight of the storm you are under will be heavy at first and hard to bear, but when you remove the weight and hand it over to God, you will feel free and so much faster. You will feel so much stronger because you are doing it not in your strength but in God's strength.

God is calling you to hand everything over to Him and He will carry it for you. I felt better when I ran my last two miles without the rucksack because I wasn't carrying it anymore, Jesus was. He will carry your rucksack too but you have to take it off first.

The last two months I continued to run with the rucksack. At the moment I didn't know why I continued to run with it, I just did. Patrick, McGwire and I had a 4 mile race coming up, it was called Finish on the 50 at the Ohio State stadium. McGwire absolutely loved this race and we were excited about it.

Ever since I started running, I've become very competitive in every race I've ever done. I've won a few races and I've placed decently in a lot of others. We ran this same race last year and I wanted to improve my time. A couple days before the race I was running down my old gravel road with my rucksack on and as I ran I started thinking about the race and I decided I wanted to run with McGwire this year. I wanted to be by his side and see the expression on his face as we ran into the Ohio State stadium.

I'm a person that likes a challenge but I needed to stick with my son this year so as I ran, I thought about it more and decided I would run with the rucksack this year. I knew this would be a true challenge for me because I only ran two miles with the rucksack on, and this race was four miles. Even though I was nervous about the length of time I would be carrying it, I still wanted to try it.

The decision was made. The only flaw I came across with this idea was, I don't like being the center of attention, and wearing the rucksack was going to bring on the attention I didn't want drawn to me. I wasn't doing this to impress people, I believe I was doing this for the purpose of this book. I believe God had me train for the last two months with the rucksack for the intentions of this book. My husband is such a great guy, so to take the attention completely off of me, he decided to run with a rucksack too, so we were in this together.

When we arrived at the race, it was packed. There were so many people there. As the time approached and the countdown was on to start the big race, I grabbed my twenty pound rucksack and strapped it on and took a big breath in. I turned to my husband and my son and gave them a fist bump and said, "We can do it!" The race began and everyone took off. People were passing us right from the start. I hated the feeling of being passed. As each person went by, I gritted my teeth and just told myself, it's ok, you're running with your son. The competitive side of me wanted to take off and go as fast as I could but I remembered I had a twenty pound rucksack on, I would never last at that speed. Besides, this race was for my son, not for me. I stayed at his pace and we ran side by side.

People were constantly passing us and I decided to put my guard down and relax. Last year when I ran in this race, everything was a blur. Honestly I don't remember too much about it because my focus was on the person in front of me and when I would find the opportunity I would go for the pass. My focus was on the win. Nothing going on around me mattered, I had tunnel vision and I wasn't going to back down for anything, not until my feet crossed that finish line.

As I ran beside my son, I watched him look around and take everything in. This made me happy and I smiled. Then I looked around and saw all the buildings and spectators. Little kids were standing on the sidelines stretching their arms out to give all the runners a high five as they crossed by. I noticed most people racing didn't acknowledge the kids as they passed by. I know when I raced, I would have passed them, because I was focused too much on the race. I shifted my way over to the kids and gave every kid on the sidelines a high five and they would celebrate jumping up and down.

This year was so different. I never experienced this side of the competition before. I can honestly say, I never enjoyed the race before. It was always miserable and I was so out of breath because I used every bit of my energy in every race. This year my eyes were fully open in this race. In the past, I was blinded by the blur of everything. We came across the water station. I never ever once took the opportunity to get a drink of water even if I desperately needed it because it would slow me down. I grabbed some water and continued to run. I looked over at McGwire and said, "I never did this before." I tried to drink it and McGwire and I laughed as I dumped most of it down the front of my shirt.

I was loving every moment of this race. I wasn't struggling this time like I usually did. I was relaxed and happy. I looked around and noticed other people were struggling. I knew people needed encouragement. We were getting towards the end of the race and people were getting tired and I didn't want to see them give up. I knew how it felt to be tired. I needed to push these people like I do in my workout classes. This is where they needed it. I started to pat people on the back as I ran by and said, "You're doing great! Hang in there, we're almost there!"

As I was running and about to finish this race, God was showing me something. In the past when I raced it was always about the win. I wanted the win, I needed the win. If I didn't do well in the race, I would be disappointed in myself. Or if I did win, it would feel good for the moment but it never kept me satisfied. It was never enough. I thought I would need more races and more wins to keep me happy but something was always missing, it always left me thirsty.

This race and the rucksack gave me a new perspective on all this. I believe today's society teaches us that you have to be first to be seen. You have to win to survive in this world. In life, we think the first person crossing that line is going to get the blessing. If we are first we are finally going to get the breakthrough we have been waiting for. We will do anything to be first. This is our generation today, if you're not first, you feel like you are not seen. No wonder all of us are fighting for attention. No wonder all of us are fighting for people to validate us. Race after race you are full of disappointment. People make you feel like you are not good enough. Year after year people start stepping all over you. After a while you feel like maybe you will never get that healing. Maybe you will stop trying and you'll stop chasing for things, you might give up because you feel like you are a blur in people's vision. You're not. That's what this world has taught us but it's so far from the truth.

I've learned today by carrying the rucksack that it's not about winning or being first, it's more than that. It took this heavy rucksack to show me this. It took the weight on my shoulders to slow me down enough to finally be able to see what it truly is about. Life is not about winning, not at all, it's about enduring. Today I didn't need a win, I needed vision, I needed to be awakened. God needed to apply weight to me to make me finally see. So when you get hit hard with a storm you have to walk through it. It might be strong and you might fall a few times because the weight is so heavy but get back up and keep going. It doesn't matter how fast you get there, it just matters that you get there. Getting there is the win, getting there is the journey, getting there is the breakthrough.

We miss so much in our lives when we run this race of life. We are running such a fast paced life and we are missing everything around us because we are chasing the win. When my son and I stepped onto the football field, we raced all the way to the fifty year yard line and he beat me. He may have won but I was carrying a rucksack and he wasn't. Maybe the people that you are competing with in life are not carrying any weight on their shoulders like you are, so stop focusing on the win and focus on the journey because you will find your healing when your foot crosses that 50 yard line.

It's not about what you have been through or what life was before you started your walk with God. God doesn't care about how you start the race as much as He cares about how you end it. We need to keep moving forward and finish the race strong. We have to endure the race and finish with God by our side and that will be the win that really matters.

# CHAPTER 43

# McGwire Found God

As time went by McGwire began to really improve, he was becoming the son that I thought I lost. He was slowly coming back to me. God was answering my prayers. I was seeing more with him. I noticed a trend of McGwire watching a show on Netflix. It was about two best friends but one was sick. She had cancer and her best friend stuck by her side the whole time. I didn't know why McGwire became so fascinated with this show but I knew he liked it because he always wanted to watch it.

One day while I was preparing supper, McGwire came up to me and was talking about that show. I said, "You really like that show don't you?" He said, "Yea, because it reminds me of you and me." I stopped what I was doing and looked back at him and said, "What do you mean bud?" He said, "It reminds me of what I've been going through." He said "I'm like the sick girl on the show and you are like her best friend. I've been sick and even though I've been mean to you," he stopped and started to cry, he took a deep breath in and continued talking with a shaky voice, "but you have not left my side. Mommy you are my best friend and I'm sorry for everything I have done. I can't control it. I want to be a good boy but sometimes I mess up because I have to fight so hard to be good."

I began to tear up hearing him say all this. I bent down to his level and said, "Pal, I know you've been fighting and I'm so proud of you. I'm so sorry you have gone through all this, I want to take this from you and I would if I could. I will never ever stop fighting for you no matter what, I promise you that." I gave him a great big hug and we both cried. I pulled him back and looked at him with his crystal blue eyes and said, "Your eyes are so blue today and you know what, you are in there buddy and I see that I'm not the only one fighting here, you are too. Keep fighting for me pal. We are in this together. You are my best friend too." I said, "McGwire, there is a God up there" as I pointed up and I said, "He is fighting with you and for you. When you have a hard time controlling everything, pray to God." He shook his head yes. He said, "Can you show me how?"

I said, "Yes pal and I took his hands and prayed there standing in the middle of the kitchen." I said, "I will tell you what. PANDAS is no longer in control of you, God is. When it tries to take control, we can stop it. Let's name it Mcfire. You can yell at it. Say enough McFire, you don't have control over me." As time went on, this helped him take control, he was able to fight it. McGwire became stronger that day, he became stronger in fighting his PANDAS and became stronger in his faith. This was the day I believe McGwire surrendered to God.

Every night the nightmares became less and less, the scary visions were barely there anymore and my made up stories turned into me reading stories of the Bible to my boys every night. Night time was no longer a nightmare, it was becoming a blessing. When I opened the Bible for the first time, I started reading the book of James and I actually started to understand it a little. God led me there because that is where God wanted us to start.

The book of James expressed a lot of McGwire's struggles and it helped him deal with all the insecurities he was dealing with. McGwire needed the book of James. I was able to comprehend it little by little because God allowed me to. If you don't understand the Bible at first, keep reading it, because God will unlock it for you as you go. Things were changing, the bad days were fading and the good days were ahead of us.

The light was finally shining into our house again. The story unfortunately doesn't end here though, because when Satan sees that you are becoming more dependent on God and less dependent on yourself, he gets scared. He will do everything in his power to stop you from making your next move.

# CHAPTER 44

# Do I Stay Or Do I Go?

There is always going to be something that stops you in your tracks and gets in your way when you are trying to get somewhere but you have to keep going even if you are scared. I know this has been a sad story. That's why it was so hard for me to write it. I want to bring some light to our story and bring some laughter into this situation.

One day, I decided to run to Paradise. This old gravel road means the world to me. It became my outlet, my safe place. Running on this road takes me to another place, into a deeper level of running. I often run there on days I feel sad, angry, and overwhelmed, but I also run there when I feel happy. This is my chance to be alone with God. I spend my time talking to God one on one with no interruptions. Running on this road gives me inner peace and it resets me to tackle whatever comes my way.

As I was running to my favorite spot on this road, I began to run down a hill and suddenly I came to a screeching stop. In the distance I noticed a calf standing in the road. This completely caught me off guard. He noticed me too. As we stared at each other, I knew the same thoughts were going through our heads. We were both scared, and not sure what to do. I debated about turning around and going back because I wasn't sure what the calf would do as I passed by. I wanted to keep going. I didn't come all this way to just turn around. This calf was messing up my run.

I had a choice to make. I either had to risk it and pass the calf and hope for the best or turn around and end my run. I decided to take a few steps forward just to see what would happen. The calf took a few steps back. I noticed at the fence in the far corner, his cow family stood there watching him. I believe they wanted him to come back. I noticed he would look at me and then he would look at them, he didn't know what to do. I decided to take a few more steps. This startled him and suddenly he began running away from me so I went with it and started to run towards him and before you knew it, we were running together. I've had a lot of running partners in my life, but I never ran with a calf before, this was the first.

The calf was running ahead of me and he kept looking back at me. I think he thought I was chasing him. I ran very slowly so I didn't get too close to him just in case he turned around and came back towards me. Suddenly he stopped in his tracks where his cow family stood and he looked at them and looked back at me. I stopped and watched him. The cows were mooing and it was as if they were cheering him on to jump back in. He was scared so I took a couple more steps towards him and he gave me one last look and he backed up and took a running leap over the fence back to his family. I sighed out of relief and started running again and as I slowly ran past them, I could tell his cow family was happy he was back and so was he.

As I ran and reached the most captivating spot of the road, I started to reflect on everything that had happened and God revealed something to me about this encounter with the calf. The message in all this really spoke to me.

The calf ran away. He found a weak spot in the fence and found a way out and he took it. He knew this was his opportunity to be able to see what laid outside of his boundaries. He was curious and that's life. We have been curious about things of the unknown at some point in our lives. As he escaped, he felt freedom but when he saw me, he realized he was in danger. He wasn't prepared for what he found outside of his boundaries. What felt like a good idea at the time for him became scary and he didn't know what to do.

God was showing me that you can't run away from all your problems because this may get you deeper into more problems. Sometimes we are called to stay and remain within the storm that we are up against, even though we feel stuck and feel limited. God revealed to me that there are always two sides of the story, you have the calf's side of the story, then you have mine.

I was the runner, I was trying to get somewhere important but something got in the way of my journey. You are going to face this at some point in your life when you are trying to get to a destination that you know you are supposed to be but the Devil will throw things in your path to stop you because he knows if you get there, you might get the breakthrough and he doesn't want that to happen. When I was running, I knew where I was headed but I wasn't prepared for an encounter with a calf, it came out of the blue without me expecting it.

A lot of problems in our lives that we may face are going to hit us like a ton of bricks and knock us off our feet. We won't see them coming. When I saw the calf, I came across a problem and I was scared to walk into it. I came this far but I saw something in my way and I wanted to go back even though I came here to move forward. Sometimes you will run into an unexpected storm that will make you want to turn around, it might make you want to quit and go back, but you have to keep moving forward even though you're scared. Going back into something you were trying to get out of is never the answer. You have to trust God is with you through the storm and He will guide you through it even though it's foggy and you're afraid.

We are going to face problems in our lives no matter what, but we have to understand that God is with us through them. Walking by faith is going to help us find the blessing ahead. I learned a lot from the encounter with the calf. In some situations, we need to stay and remain where we are and in other situations we need to move forward.

I believe God was revealing to me that the calf represented my son while I represented myself as the runner. When McGwire was sick, he wanted to run away from everything. He went into hiding all the time. My son wanted to escape the storm he was trapped in. In his mind running from his family was the answer. He was ashamed of everything. He didn't want us to see him like he was so he chose to leave and be with my mom, but choosing to run away created more problems and more trauma. All he needed to do was stay. We would have given him the love and compassion he needed. We would have endured it with him but instead he ran and pushed us away. We were calling him back but he was too scared to come back. The problems he faced outside were too much to bear and finally he came back and we were able to fight this together.

I believe I represent myself as the runner in this story. When McGwire was sick I felt like I couldn't move at times. I felt numb and paralyzed because I was scared for my son. I missed him and all I wanted to do was help him but I couldn't. I constantly focused on the worst case scenarios of what could happen just like I did when I came across the calf. When McGwire was sick, God was calling me to get up and move; to face my fears and move into the present moment, to focus on right now and not on the future. God was calling me to move forward and help my son find his healing. I was scared of the calf and what might happen when I passed him and I was also scared for my son and what would happen in the future.

We have to quit looking so far ahead and walk through the storm because there is always a rainbow waiting for you on the other side. My point is, it's really easy to cross those boundaries but it's hard to make your way back through them. When you are called to remain in the storm, then stay and endure it but if you are called to move, then go and walk into it. Sometimes when you make your next move and it brings you closer to God, you become a threat to Satan.

When you stay close with God, Satan has no power over you and he becomes stuck. He may keep trying to hit you with new problems, but it doesn't work when you are focused on God. So Satan does what he does best. He studies you and he finds those weak spots. He looks for your vulnerabilities. If he can't find anything new to hit you with, he will hit you where he has already hit you once before. He will go back to your past wounds, he finds those wounds that aren't quite healed yet, those wounds that are still raw and exposed: that's where he hits again. He will find where all the trauma already lies and go in for the attack. He makes sure that he takes it to the next level. He intensifies the attack.

The Devil knew my fears. He knew I was scared we would go back to square one, that we would have to start all over again with all the chaos, all the nightmares, and all of the tantrums. I didn't want to go back, I wanted to keep moving forward but unfortunately that's exactly what happened to us, we found ourselves in round two of this battle of PANDAS.

# CHAPTER 45

# It's Back Again

Christmas was around the corner, again. I tried to make Christmas special this year because I didn't want us to hold onto the memories of Christmas last year when he was diagnosed with PANDAS. McGwire still had his ups and downs. We still had days when he had flares but he was making great progress.

It was about a week before Christmas and McGwire got sick again. It all started with Pink eye in both eyes and he had a bad cough. I had no choice but to call his doctors office in Columbus and ask what we should do? They said, "Take him to his regular doctor and they will have to look at him and switch his antibiotic if he has an infection." I hated to do this. McGwire has been so healthy this whole year, he hasn't been sick at all because of being on this antibiotic and all the added supplements. I didn't feel comfortable taking him off his medication and they warned me that this could change things, it was a risky move but for him to fight the infection he currently had, they had to make the switch.

I took him to a nurse practitioner at his regular doctor's office. She said he had a viral infection. She never treated a child with PANDAS before. She was scared to make the switch but she knew this needed to be done. After the switch, McGwire started into a full blown flare. He couldn't come out of it. This time was different. It was worse. The fears he once had were back but they were intensified. This flare that we were in lasted all day long. He got to the point he would lay on the couch and scream. When he closed his eyes he saw dark images, scary monsters and the fear set in.

The big difference this time was he let me in, he allowed me to comfort him, to hold him, reassuring him it was going to be ok. At least I had that, but we were back into nightmare mode again. As long as I stuck by his side he handled it, when I walked away for a few minutes the torment would be back and the screaming would start again. I couldn't leave his side, he wouldn't let me, nor did I want to. This took a toll on the whole family again.

Doing this day after day affected me mentally. I was emotional and mentally exhausted. I was so consumed in all this and so was he. I was glad he let me hold him this time but the images were so much worse. I had to get him through this flare, I had to ride this wave with him. My husband noticed this, he saw me struggling mentally. Christmas came and went and it was again not a pleasant Christmas. McGwire's virus went away with the new antibiotic so we switched him back on his original one.

At this point I hadn't been out of the house for days, which was not like me because I am a person that is highly active and Patrick knew what this was doing to me. He knew I needed to get out of the house for a little bit and go for a run. My husband knew I needed a moment just to breathe and absorb what's going on. I needed fresh air, I needed sunshine because I was living in the dark. My son needed me though and I needed to be there with him, but I also needed to reset myself.

My husband came into the house one day and saw us laying on the couch. It was a nice day. This was a weird winter. We had spring-like days and this was one of them. Patrick knew we needed to get outside a little and get some fresh air. It would be good for all of us. He saw the stress on my face. I got up off the couch and Patrick gave me a big hug and I teared up and he said, "Cass, things are going to be ok." I said, "Really, then why are we going through this again?" He said, "I don't know but we need to get out and enjoy this nice day, that might help him. You haven't run for a long time. I think you need that." I said, "I do but McGwire needs me." He said, "I got McGwire, I got the boys. I will take them to Mcdonalds and pick up lunch while you run and we'll eat outside and shoot the new bow and arrow that McGwire got for Christmas." I looked over at McGwire and said "Are you sure, you think he will be ok?" He said, "Yes, you need to get out, and do something." I looked outside and said, "You're right, I do."

My boys got in the car and I waved goodbye to them and put my earbuds in and I took off running. I had a sense of guilt go through me, I missed my boys already. I didn't want them to leave. My emotions were all over the place. I felt sad because I missed my kiddos. I had been wrapped up with them for days. I felt lonely without my boys, but running always left a sense of peace and it filled me with joy. I decided to run down our road outside of my house. I breathed in the fresh air, I absorbed the sunshine, and admired the trees and the birds. It was so beautiful. I felt weak because I hadn't been up for days. I've been laying on the couch with McGwire all this time.

As I ran my mind was going crazy. I never really got to absorb all this or evaluate things or even process them. I needed this run, I needed to release my emotions. I needed to let them go and not hold them in. I held my tears back so I could be strong for my son but I couldn't hold them back now as I ran down the road. I felt the tears build up with every step I took. I felt the agony my son was in. I felt the pain of what he was going through. I hated it because I wanted to take it from him, but all I could do was just lay with him and watch him go through it.

As I ran I realized I was just going through the motions. I was paralyzed when he became sick. I couldn't thrive if he couldn't. I couldn't do it without him, he needed to get better. I don't want to go through this nightmare again. I wanted it to be over. I thought it was over but It was back. My sadness quickly turned to anger. I was mad that he had to go through this at such a young age. I was mad that he was going through this all over again.

As I ran, I had my earbuds in and a song came on. I had heard this song before but I never listened to the words before until then. The words were speaking to me. The song was called, "You Say," by Lauren Daigle. She started the song by saying, "I keep fighting voices in my mind that say I'm not enough, every single lie tells me I will never measure up." I continued to listen carefully to her words. She went on by saying, "Am I more than just the sum of every high and every low, remind me again just who I am because I need to know."

These lyrics were like my son was talking to me, these were his feelings, his words, every word spoke of his struggles. It went on saying, "You say I am loved when I don't feel a thing, you say I am strong when I think I am weak, and you say I am held when I am falling short. And when I say I don't belong, oh you say I am yours, and I believe." I was lost in my music, lost in the powerful words that were being sung. I was lost in my emotions. I was lost in my run, as I ran, I felt God's presence. It was as if He was opening these words up to me, revealing my son's emotions and revealing mine.

This allowed me to understand what McGwire was dealing with. My son was struggling but so was I, I felt what he felt. I began to run faster and faster, one foot after the other. I was going through the motions but I was flooding with emotions. My heart ached, my breathing became struggled. My legs became heavy. My arms became weak. I became paralyzed. I couldn't move but I was still moving. I was emotionally numb. My legs were about to give out on me and suddenly I stopped and dropped to my knees and started crying on the side of the road.

As soon as I dropped, a car approached me. I wanted to get up but I couldn't. I just held my head down in shame hoping they would pass by. The person pulled over, stopped and opened the door and stepped out walking towards me. With embarrassment, I looked up, tears flooded my eyes and I saw tears form in hers, it was my mom. I was relieved it was her. It was her sweet face. I cried harder. I allowed myself to release my tears with her standing there. She bent down to my level and hugged me. She hugged me so tight like she used to when I was little and I would fall and scrape my leg, or on the nights I was awakened from a bad dream. She held me, without hesitation. Sweat was pouring from me, she didn't care, she still held me. She cried and I cried harder. I let it all out. My Mom wiped the tears from my eyes and said, "Cassie, it's going to be ok. God's got this. This too shall pass."

She stood up and helped me off the ground and said, "Come here." I did what she said. She said, "Scream." I said, "What?" She said, "Scream, let it out." I said, "Will people hear me?" She said, "Who cares, just release this Cass, it will feel good. I will do it with you, on the count of three. One. Two. Three." And we screamed. I could have screamed louder but I felt stupid, but it did feel good when I did it. She hugged me again and asked if I wanted a ride and I said, "No I'm going to finish my run. Thank you Mom, you made me feel so much better."

She got back in her car and smiled at me and waved and I placed my earbuds back in my ears and ran back home.

When I got home I sat down on the porch and my family pulled in and both of my boys hopped out of the car and gave me a big hug. McGwire was full of smiles. He said, "We got McDonald's and Daddy said we could eat and then shoot my new bow and arrow." I smiled and said, "Yes, let's do it." God gave me that run, that song, and that opportunity so I could release everything. God allowed my Mom to find me broken and down on my knees. She was there for me at the right place and at the right time.

Later that day I took McGwire to Paradise road and I told him to scream and we screamed together. McGwire began to improve again. I'm not going to say McGwire was one hundred percent yet. We had a ways to go. We still had our ups and downs with him. It was a process but as time grew our faith grew and he did get better.

# CHAPTER 46

# The Picture

A couple years after McGwire was diagnosed with PANDAS, he was doing really well and making great progress. We were scheduled for a follow up with his doctor in Columbus. They went through a series of questions like they did in the past. As I went through the questions I realized the things McGwire once struggled with were so much better. As she evaluated things she said, "McGwire I think you are healed. I think it's time to take you off the antibiotic and remove some of these supplements." She looked at me and said, "McGwire is now considered in remission."

My mom was with us that day and I was so happy I began to tear up but held it together. I gave McGwire a big hug and he smiled the biggest smile you can imagine. God answered our prayers, we were past this. He finally won this battle with the help of God. We couldn't have done it without God. As we waited to be dismissed, McGwire said he needed to use the bathroom, so I walked him there and waited.

As I stood there waiting for him, there was a nurses station right beside me and out of the corner of my eye a picture caught my attention. I glanced at it for a second and then looked away and something hit me. I drifted back to the picture again and began to walk closer. I squinted my eyes to get a deeper look at it. Something rushed deep inside me as I fixated my eyes on this picture.

This was a picture of a man. I found myself drawing closer and closer so I could really get a good look at this picture to make sure I was seeing it right. The man had mid length, brown, shaggy hair with a short brown beard. I studied the man's face and I looked into his eyes. He had deep chocolate brown eyes. I looked deeper into his eyes, and studied him carefully. I've seen those captivating eyes before. They had a magnetizing pull to them.

I continued to look at this picture searching for something in the man's eyes. It felt like time was standing still, it all happened in slow motion. It was like I wasn't standing in a doctor's office any longer. I was in my own world. I knew this man's face from somewhere, but where? It was so familiar to me. I knew those eyes, I've looked into them before. Then it hit me like a ton of bricks. I came back to earth. I came out of my trance unlocking my eyes from the man's eyes.

The picture of the man wasn't just any man. This was the man in my dream. This was Jesus. The exact same Jesus I saw in my dream. The only difference was He wasn't crying anymore but I was. The tear wasn't streaming from His eye like it was in my dream, but tears were streaming from mine. I wasn't crying because I was sad. I was crying because I knew that dream had led me here. Jesus led me to this office. I knew we were on the right path. I never once related my dream to preparing me for McGwire getting sick. Not even for a moment did I ever break this dream down enough to know it led me here.

To be honest, I forgot about the dream. The dream was blurred by the battle we were under. I never once related anything to this dream until this very moment. This dream was the beginning of our storm. Jesus sent a dream to prepare me for what was getting ready to come. That dream was followed by a sudden urge that I had to quit my job. That dream led me to step off one path and walk on a new one. I walked away from being a mammographer just in time so I could be there for my son when he got sick. I was there to help him fight through this battle. God knew I would have not been able to work when McGwire was sick so he had me quit right before McGwire got sick.

Being a mammographer was a chapter in my life and it was never wasted. It was there to guide me to my new path. It was the stepping stone to get me to where I am now. It prepared me to walk into my true purpose. My gym has always been the dream, but it took a battle for me to make that move. It took a real, actual dream to find my true dream, my gym. The reality is my son got sick but my son getting sick was the new direction. The storm was hard but it created a blessing.

It was the new path.

My son was the sacrifice. I would have never taken that sudden turn on that gravel road on my own will because I never would have believed it was possible. That backroad looked too unfamiliar. Those hills looked too big to climb. But after you face a big storm like we did, those hills didn't look too bad after all. The strength we gained after this storm has given us victory. I learned on this journey that nothing is impossible when God is in it. This was our last appointment with McGwire's doctor. The doctor told us McGwire was healed. My son was cleansed. This sickness no longer had control over him, God did. But it took me letting go of McGwire and handing him over to God. I had to let God step in because this storm was too big for me to carry McGwire through it, we needed a Savior to clear the way.

This doesn't mean we stop fighting. I never quit fighting for my son. This just means let God take control and follow him and He will lead you and show you how to fight. God saved us. He heard my prayers and He answered them when the time was right. God is going to answer your prayers too. Keep praying and keep knocking, and eventually in God's perfect timing, He will answer your prayers. Just trust Him. This might be a new chapter in your life and it may be a long chapter that is hard for you to get through.

My advice is to keep fighting because you are about to get to the good part. You're about to take a sudden turn and you will finally find your blessing. That breakthrough is on its way. After we got home we told Patrick about McGwire being healed and he couldn't believe it, he was so happy. My son was healed and we were done fighting the long hard battle but for some reason, even though McGwire was healed, I began to struggle and I began to fall back into that pit again. Why?

# CHAPTER 47

# Why Did He Get Better
# But I Got Worse?

Writing this story was hard for me. It was so painful to relive this story all over again. It hurts but it was worth all those tears I shed. At the end of day, I don't regret writing this story because if I can help another person, even if it is only you that reads it, it was worth every tear because you are worth it. Your battle that you are fighting right now will be over. Your battle also will be your story to share. It will be your testimony to spread to others so they know that they can defeat their giants like you have.

I had moments when McGwire was sick that I completely lost it and broke down. I also had moments that I remained strong for my son, I had to. I had to learn to be tough even when I didn't feel tough. It wasn't until my son got better that I found myself getting worse.

Why is that? Why did I get worse when he was getting better? It doesn't make sense. I should have gotten better too. In a sense I did get better. My joy came back as I saw McGwire improve. My faith grew during this time in my life but as time went on I backslid and found myself going back into that pit. Why? I believe the answer to that is, God gave me His strength that I needed at that moment to help my son get better. God will always supply just enough strength that you need for the battle.

I believe when McGwire showed improvement, I could back down from the fight. I could let my guard down and unclench my fists. I could finally let go of what I was holding onto but when I did, I felt weak. I believe this is just like a soldier in a battle. He remains strong in the battle because he was trained for it but when he gets home, he has time to think, then the memories come. The battle is over physically but the battle goes on mentally. That was me, I had time to think and time wasn't good for me. Time was never on my side so I made sure I didn't have any time, so I became busy. I never left room for gaps in my schedule because in those gaps were all the anxiety I carried and I never wanted to go there, so I avoided time.

I would overload my schedule so I could shut down my thinking and the trauma that went along with it. I didn't realize what I was doing but I realize it now. I was running away from the pain, not physically but mentally. I never wanted time to catch up to me because if it did, it wasn't good. When McGwire got better, I fell apart because I could. I found myself in a deep depression and I found myself sick from anxiety. I allowed it to take control of me and I should have never let it take control.

I started to get scared and it's ok to be scared, but never let the fear drive and direct you because it will take you to all the wrong places. I had a fear that McGwire's sickness would come back and we would have to face round three of this battle, and I knew I didn't have a round three in me. We all have insecurities. Our insecurities are the chains that we are bound to. The storms we face sometimes can put us in these chains. I know when my son was sick, I locked myself tight in these chains. McGwire is now 13 years old and he is healed, I really do believe that. Sometimes McGwire has an attitude like a typical teenager does but I would always relate it to him being sick again.

I know McGwire is cleansed, but these chains I am bound to, convinces me that these behaviors are symptoms of PANDAS. At times I get a fear that rushes through me allowing me to believe that we are not dealing with an attitude, we are back into our storm full throttle. I often found myself putting my guards up when I didn't need to. I was always ready for the battle, the battle that was over.

If it was over, why was I still fighting? I knew I needed to find a way to overcome this because I was constantly throwing my son's sickness in his face whenever he acted out. This wasn't good for him. I wasn't allowing him to heal because of my insecurities. These chains I was in was keeping McGwire and I both bound to this sickness. I didn't want to tell you all this about me but I needed to because I don't want you to do what I did. It wasn't healthy and because of what I did,

I have carried this trauma longer than I needed to.

You have to let go. God didn't intend for me to be bound to these chains, He just wants me to use them. My advice to you is don't avoid the thoughts, deal with them. Speak them to a trusted friend, to your husband, your mom. Write them down, like I am today. Don't run from them, because they will eventually catch up to you. Don't tuck them away in a little box like I did, because one day you will have to open that box and it won't be good when you do.

I opened that box when I started writing this book. The emotions I had avoided for so long exploded. I tucked all my feelings away and never dealt with them until I sat down and started writing this book. That's why it took me so long to write it. I couldn't do it at first. It was too hard, because I never felt these emotions for a long time and honestly, I didn't like them. I kept them hidden. I constantly got mad and gave up over and over again on this book until now. I said I am going to do this, I won't give up because I have you, the person who needs to read this. If I can help you then it was worth every moment I broke down slamming the laptop shut.

I asked McGwire if I could write this book. I wanted his approval because this is his story. He said, "Yes, absolutely." He said he wants his story to be heard. He wants to help others overcome their battle too. As I started writing, McGwire started to realize what the sickness that tormented him did to me. I never showed that side to him before. He saw me cry as I wrote this book. This became a concern to me because he started to feel guilty.

I told him, please don't feel guilty. I tried my best to shield him from my tears but I couldn't because I had to release the tears that I never had until now. That's what this book did for me. I couldn't hold them back anymore. This book has allowed me to let go of those burdens and pick up the pen God wanted me to use to heal you, but in return to heal me. This book has been good for me, but not McGwire necessarily, because he started to blame himself. I didn't want that, I needed him to know that he wasn't the reason for my tears. I wanted him to know that when he saw me cry, it wasn't his fault. I didn't want him to think he was the reason I struggled.

I couldn't let him take the blame. I didn't want him to tie all this to being his fault. He saw himself as the one who was sick, the one who pushed me away, the one who was lost. He saw himself as the problem, in reality he was the result. He constantly hugged me and said he was sorry for everything he did. I constantly told him it's ok, don't blame yourself. I didn't want this burden on him, I didn't want him to feel he had to be the one to wipe my tears away. I was the one who was supposed to do that for him.

I wanted McGwire to know he had it all wrong. He had it all backwards. Yes I cried because it hurt reliving this again. Thinking back on these times was painful and yes I may have shed a few tears but those tears were because I loved him so much. I wanted McGwire to know he wasn't the reason I cried.

He is the reason I live. He is the reason I am strong today. The reason I dropped to my knees and surrendered. He is the reason I fight. He is the reason why my family is stronger than they ever have been before. He is the reason Larkin knows God at such a young age. He is the reason we are now in a church. He is the reason I found running. He is the reason I found my new path. He is the reason I'm living my dream, my purpose. He is the reason why someone may cry on my shoulder and I am able to comfort them because I know what it feels like to hurt. He is the reason I will never give up, he showed me how to fight back.

I am who I am today and we are who we are as a family because of McGwire. I am a changed person for the good because of him. He took one for the team, he was the sacrifice. God chose him and used him to save us. God used an eight year old boy to save a family and I am hoping God is using my computer and our testimony to save your family. McGwire isn't the reason I cry or the reason I struggle, but he is the reason I'm strong.

That all being said brings me to this very important question. Do we want to forget all of this and let all of these memories go? Do we walk away from all this pain and leave it all behind us and never look back or Do we want to remember this, and use our storm to help others? Do we use our testimony to give people hope? Do we show our scars to remind us that we survived and we can survive again?

I find myself caught between two barriers, do we forget and let go or do we remember and hold on? I find myself wanting to bury these memories and never look back. I want to remove these chains once and for all but yet I want to use these chains to help people. What do we do? I want this behind our family, I don't want to live in the past, I want to carry on into the future. I don't want us chained up to something that will hold us back from where God is leading us.

This is why I struggle so much writing each painful word of this story but at the same time, you need this story for hope. I need this story to heal and McGwire needs this story to show people what strength looks like. If we leave this memory in the dust and never look back, will we remember what brought us to our knees? Will pride set in? Will we forget what God did for us and all the sacrifices it took? Will we lose the fight inside of us? Will we lose the strength we gained from our battle? Will the struggle be worth it if we forget everything and bury it? Will that thorn in our side serve its purpose?

My son and I both live the same testimony, but we live it from different outlooks, I lived it from the outside looking in and he lived it from the inside looking out. I can't feel what he feels or see what he sees. I didn't live with the sickness inside me like he did. He can't see what I went through trying to help him and fight for him. We both lived the same story but in reverse or backwards. His heartache is mine and my heartache is his but we suffer differently.

How do we heal? How do we get past all this? We need to loosen the chains and shake those shackles off and break free from that prison we were trapped in. but yet we need to pick up those chains and use them. I promised McGwire when we got through this battle and the fight was over, we were going to help other families so no other child had to suffer without knowing what direction to go. This is the journey we are on now with telling our story of this backroad blessing.

Our chains are loose and we are no longer bound to them because God broke us free. I will use these chains for the rest of my life so I can show people that they are heavy, but if you use them you will become stronger. You will save people by revealing the power these chains hold.

One thing I do know is God wants me to write this book for you, because you are hurting inside, your feelings are raw, your pain is real. Yes, I wrote this book for you but God revealed to me that I also wrote this book for me. I wrote it for clarity, for closure and for healing. God wanted me to break those chains once and for all and I wasn't going to do it by tucking the pain away. I had to use the weapon He equipped me with and that was the power of the pen, but it was my choice whether to pick it up.

The healing came with the power of each word I wrote and these words broke each link of the chain I was bound to. Each sentence I wrote helped me break free from that prison I locked myself in. Each paragraph I finally shook those shackles off my feet. Each chapter brought me freedom from those raw emotions and trauma that was trapped inside. I was free from the sickness that laid dormant inside my son. This book has taught me that my son is now healed, he is cleansed because of the grace of God.

This book has allowed me to break those chains once and for all and trust that God cleansed McGwire. This book has allowed me to put these insecurities to rest. We are all tied to chains but we have the choice to break free. Satan is constantly after us, whispering in our ears, trying to convince us that we will never break those chains.

I am here to tell you he is wrong, he is a liar, don't believe him. God is a chain breaker, He can do the impossible. Satan intended these chains to be used as a trap but God intended these chains to be used as victory. Victory is yours. If you just stand up those chains will loosen and fall off, but remember to pick them up and use them.

# CHAPTER 48

# He's Healed

I am so blessed and happy to say that McGwire is now healed. My family is healed, we are now stronger as a family but stronger in our faith too. We have changed but for the better. What we went through was hard but in a way I am thankful for it because I have seen blessing after blessing because of it.

I want everyone reading this to know that McGwire isn't a bad kid, it was just the conditions PANDAS caused him to have. He wasn't that way before he was sick, and he is not that way now. McGwire is the sweetest, most compassionate boy that I know. He is so amazing to me. I'm not just saying that because he is my son, I'm saying it because it's true. God did something in him through this time of his sickness and the outcome has been great.

Football has always been McGwire's dream but when he was sick, I had no choice but to remove him from the football team. This was hard on him but he was understanding. Through myself becoming busy, I became the cross country coach and he ended being our very first elementary runner and due to this we created the very first elementary team for Morgan Elementary. McGwire ran cross country all the way up to his sixth grade year.

He came up to me his sixth grade year and asked if he could play football. He said, "Mom, I will be fine, God will protect me. Don't worry anymore, I'm healed, please, you know how important football is to me, and I'm ready, are you ready mom?" "He said trust God." I said, "I trust Him and I trust He will protect you." In McGwire's sixth grade year, he played football and I told him he could quit cross country country. He said, "No Mom, I'm doing both. I started this cross country team and I will not quit until I finish my last year with them."

McGwire completed his sixth grade year as one of our top cross country runners and the quarterback of his football team. Currently he is the lead quarterback of the junior high football team. I told him I wanted him to focus on football and not to worry about cross country so I stepped down as the coach so I could watch him play football. Everyday before he goes onto the field he thanks God for everything and points up to the sky because he knows who is watching down on him. Philippians 4:13 is his favorite verse, "I can do all things through Christ who strengthens me." He wears a chain wrapped around his neck with this verse, he carries it with him everywhere he goes.

Our bond is closer than it ever has been. McGwire doesn't have much memory of all of this and Larkin has no memory of any of it. This is a blessing to me that they don't remember the battle we went through. It's all foggy to McGwire but it was all real, so real. This is God's grace. McGwire does know he went through something and he knew Who pulled him out of it. He knows where his strength comes from. I give God praise for His glory in answering our prayers.

As I told you, I recently discovered McGwire and I have old mini books that we use to write. He would always draw the pictures and I would look at them and would create a story to go along with his artwork. I was the author, he was the illustrator. That was step one to God's process.

I look back on those days when McGwire and I used to write books together. Little did I know this was a set up for today. As I look at the books we made together, I realized God prepared us back then to write our story. He knew this battle was coming and He prepared me to tell stories to McGwire as he laid in bed with the torment inside his head. That was step two.

God will slowly take you step by step in guiding through His purpose. He prepared us for this battle to write a bigger story. A story that was bigger than a few pieces of blank paper stapled together. He prepared us for the story we will write together today.

This book you read was step three, the finished result to His perfect plan. McGwire was the one who was sick, he was the one who suffered, he is the one I write about today. He is in the illustration of this book and I am the author. I lived this story from the outside and McGwire lived this story from the inside.

God revealed to me recently it wasn't by any accident that I put my pen down. It was by purpose that I shut my computer down for a year. He revealed to me that at the time He wasn't ready for me to write it, my journey wasn't over, there was more to the story. He had to strengthen my spirit more and give me more stories to write.

He showed me that I wasn't ready to write it yet and you weren't ready to read it. I had to put my pen down and wait because this book is for you and your storm hasn't arrived yet, not until now. If I finished on my own deadline, when I wanted to finish, then it would be too early because you wouldn't be struggling yet. You wouldn't have a need for this book. I've been waiting for you.

I know God used this book for me to heal but it's also for your healing too. When God brought me back to writing again it was because this was the right time. I had to start over fresh. The journey goes on, our testimony lives, so I can spread it to help others, so I can help you. But now the time has arrived and unfortunately that means your storm is here and you are probably scared like I was.

I know the storm you are under right now feels like the worst thing you've ever been through. My advice to you is hang in there. Don't give up, keep walking through it. Keep fighting your way through the storm and if you get weary on the way ask for God to step in and carry you through it. God will always meet you where you are. He will always dig you out of that pit when you get stuck, you just have to ask. The doctors will help, friends will step in, finding an outlet is needed but God is the ultimate healer and He will show you the way. Let Him clear out anything standing in the way of you and your blessing.

All storms come to an end and a lot of times they end with rainbows. Your rainbow is coming but you have to rise up even when it's hard to stand. Like I had to keep fighting when it hurt and it still stings a little, but it's the sting that heals. It's these battles that strengthen you for the next chapter. You're going to get past this and when you do you will finally see where God was leading you.

The path to get there isn't always easy, it can be disguised as an old rugged backroad but when you get there you will discover the new you. The you that you have been searching for. The stronger version of you, the you that you have been hiding behind, God is revealing to you, the you that God has always seen and you haven't discovered until now.

God gave me a weapon and it was the power of my pen. When I picked up the pen, I wrote McGwire's story, our testimony. We have scars that remind us of our battle. These scars remind me of God's grace and when I look back I realize the Devil didn't win, my son won, my family won, God won and He always has victory.

As I run down this old rugged road with McGwire by my side, I give him a fist bump and I say we can do it, because we can do all things through Christ who strengthens us. You can do it too. As my mom would say to me and I will say to you "This too shall pass."

Through all this, McGwire has taught me the power of compassion and positivity. He has shown me the true meaning of bravery. One thing is, people will question God and say why me? I know I did and it's ok if you do. We need to come to grips that God has His reasons and we need to trust the process. God needed us to fall to our knees and hand everything over to Him. God wants to use us and He wants to use you too.

McGwire has been my hero through all this. After everything he has been through, he has never played the victim and let this diagnosis control him. He knows who God is and he knows that his diagnosis will never limit his horizons. He knows there is never any mountain too big for him to climb when God is climbing it with him. This is McGwire's story, this is the long, winding road we took, but we got there and you will too.

Use the weapons God has equipped you with. Use the strength you have, even if it's not much because God will give you the rest. Find your outlet and don't give up, you are almost there! Remember it's in the struggle that makes you stronger. This is McGwire's story, this is my family's testimony and this is my backroad blessing.

# Acknowledgments

F irst and foremost I would like to thank God for chasing after me and helping me find my way into his loving arms. Thank you God for healing my son and bringing my family back together stronger than ever.

I would like to thank my husband, Patrick, for believing in me when I didn't. Thank you for supporting me through all my hard decisions that God was leading me towards. Thank you for never letting me give up, even when I wanted to. Thank you for pushing me towards my dreams and helping me bring them alive.

I want to thank my mom, Teresa Weiner and my dad, Mike Weiner, for sticking with us through this dark time of our lives and being there for my son when I couldn't be. Thank you for taking me to church as a young girl. Thank you for showing me how to pray and pushing me towards the One greater than all my problems, thank you for leading me to God. Thank you for showing me my way.

I want to thank Larkin for being my little baby boy that was always there for me to hold. Thank you for comforting me through this rough time in our lives and thank you for letting me rock you everyday in our rocking chair. Thank you for all the things you have shown me that God has done within you. You have known God for most of your life now and I'm so grateful for that. I know God will use you, he has great plans for you and I'm so proud of the little boy you have become.

I want to thank McGwire for being the one who took the sacrifice for the family to find God. I want to thank him for fighting back for his life and not giving up. God chose him and he is the reason I dropped to my knees and surrendered to God. Thank you for allowing me to write this book and letting me share your testimony. I know God also has plans for you, I see big things in your future and I couldn't be any more proud of the young man you are becoming.

I want to thank my workout family and all the people that I train. I couldn't do any of this without you. You have all been a big part of my life and I am so thankful for that. Thank you for sticking with me through it all. Thank you Angie Vorhies, Heather Gillespie, and Kaleb Wilkins for being the foundation of my gym, you were all my start and you never gave up on me. We all learned everything together and you all showed me my path and helped me get there. You were the ones who held me together through the hardest time of my life. Thank you for putting a smile on my face when I couldn't produce one on my own. Thank you for being there for me though all this. Thank you Angie for taking all the wonderful pictures of my favorite road, Paradise, for the cover of this book.

I want to thank Misti Clemens for being the teacher that she didn't have to be, for going above and beyond for my son. For understanding what we were going through. Thank you for taking the time and helping him do his homework, I know you felt like it was just a simple thing you did but you did more than you will ever know. Thank you for being the great teacher that you are and I am so glad you have joined my workout family and are still a big part of my family's life.

I want to thank everyone who had a part in helping me finally bring this book alive. I want to thank two of my very close friend's and proof-readers Judy Ratcliff and Bobbi Parsons for taking the time to read my book and help me through the process. I couldnt have done it without either of you. I appreciate the constructive feedback, valuable suggestions and insightful comments. I want to thank Melody Rittberger for all your useful advice and suggestions helping me design the layout of this book and prepare it for publishing.

I want to thank my church family at Cornerstone Church. I want to thank Kathy Bebout for inviting me to go with you to church and being such a great friend to me. Thank you to the church for helping me find a great connection group to do Bible studies and helping me grow in my faith. Thank you Pastor Steve for guiding me through the process on how to publish my book and making me feel welcome and part of the family at church.

Thank you to all my readers for taking your time to sit down and read my book. My goal is that you learn who God really is and that you use what I taught you in this book to help bring some light into your life. This battle you are under can also be your Backroad Blessing!

www.ingramcontent.com/pod-product-compliance
Lightning Source LLC
Chambersburg PA
CBHW030921090426
42737CB00007B/269